A COLLECTION OF
UNREAL THINGS

A COLLECTION OF UNREAL THINGS

Andrew-Mark Thompson

First published in England by:
Telos Publishing Ltd, 139 Whitstable Road, Canterbury, Kent CT2 8EQ
www.telos.co.uk

Telos Publishing Ltd values feedback. Please e-mail any comments you
might have about this book to: feedback@telos.co.uk.

ISBN: 978-1-84583-219-3

In case any reader is in doubt, this book is a celebratory spoof/pastiche, and
none of the products pictured within has ever been produced or placed on sale.

Printed and bound in the UK by Short Run Press, Exeter, Devon.

British Library Cataloguing in Publication Data.
A catalogue record for this book is available from the British Library.

DEDICATION

'It means getting the steps!'

This is for Adam.

His biting sense of humour was always a constant source of inspiration and enjoyment. He was taken from the world suddenly and far too soon.

ACKNOWLEDGEMENTS

Huge thanks to the two Steves – Steve Hardy and Steve Hatcher – who have put up with me trying out gags on them to see if they are actually funny. So you can blame them if this book isn't a barrel of laughs.

I'd also like to thank my Twitter followers for their constant tweets and retweets and breaking all the social media rules by being kind and nice – even when they don't agree with me.

Last (and by no means least), a huge acknowledgement for the patience and support that David J Howe and Stephen James Walker have sent in my general direction. This is my first book, and I'm quite a naïve amateur when it comes to prepping something like this for publishing. Both gentlemen have put up with my queries, delays and excuses and this book is the result of their understanding. Thanks, guys.

ANDREW-MARK THOMPSON
@andydrewz

FOREWORD

I have been researching and writing about DOCTOR WHO for many years now, and my investigations have taken me into all corners of this magnificent show and how it has been presented and merchandised over the years.

I thought I knew all there was to know ... but then adverts started appearing online for merchandise items I had never heard of ... dolls of the Doctors to collect ... magazines missing from my collection ... And then I realised that this was a whole new world of *Doctor Who* to explore.

In the revamped and revitalised series of *Doctor Who*, the tenth Doctor speaks of 'the could-have-been King with his army of Meanwhiles and Never-weres,' and this is the world that Andrew-Mark Thompson inhabits. He is the true could-have-been King, apparently pulling from a wormhole in his cellar a multitude of never-weres, dragged kicking and screaming through the void and the rift between times ... In that otherworld where *Doctor Who* began as a radio serial just after the War, there were Denys Fisher action figures of Jamie and Soldeed; there was a first anniversary celebration of the show at the Vicarage Garden in Mayfield; and there was a Build-A-Dalek partwork. *Doctor Who*'s first episode was launched with its very own *Radio Times* cover, and was discussed across the airwaves on a panel show. There were books, magazines and videos galore, all taking a sideways glance at the show ... There were collectible items of all shapes and sizes ... And on the far side of the wormhole, BBC Studios tried to retrofit the thirteenth Doctor onto all past merchandise ...

Here we have a book packed with these incredible items from beyond the rim of reality ... things we would have all coveted, had they been produced in our universe ... but were consigned to an alternate multiverse until Andrew-Mark discovered the portal in his basement through which he could access all these seemingly lost, and, to us, completely imaginary, gems from *Doctor Who*'s forgotten history.

Join us for a romp through the could-have-happened and the might-have-been ... and just keep telling yourself ... somewhere, in some strange dimension, this is a *Doctor Who* fan's reality!

DAVID J HOWE

DOCTOR WHO HISTORIAN AND COLLECTOR

The B.B.C. presents

Dr.WHO

Astounding Adventures in Science and Excitement in SOUND

The famous film actor **BILLY HARTNELL** who lends his voice to the mysterious science boffin called *Dr Who.*

THE FAMOUS BRITISH RADIO HERO

Forty 15 minute dramatic presentations of daring action now available on 78rpm recording discs for re-broadcast to your valuable listeners across the radio airways.

1. THE CASE OF THE SHOOTING STAR

A mysterious space projectile crashes on Windborough Plains. It contains an unknown indestructable element that Brigadier Sir Edward Leatherbridge thinks will contribute towards the Allied war effort. But enemy agents have other ideas and kidnap his wife Lady Catherine and hold her to ransom. Dr.WHO is assigned to the case. Can he stop the enemy agents in time and rescue the girl?

2. INVASION FROM SPACE

Mysterious airship sightings in the Home Counties are investigated by Dr.WHO and his young batman. It turns out they are rocketships from the planet Saturn. The Sattans are observing the war. Dr.WHO must prove to them that the Allies are on the side of the good. But enemy agents kidnap his adopted niece Gwen Forman and use her in a deadly blackmail plot that could spell doom for the free world.

3. DR WHO AND THE SECRET WEAPON

Professor Brett has invented a new machine which he thinks will win Britain the war. It's called a 'computor', and uses advanced radio waves to take control of aircraft. Enemy agents kidnap his niece Pollyanna in order to convince Brett to betray his comrades and hand over the secret 'computor' plans, which they plan to use to turn RAF pilots into slave zombies of the Third Reich.

4. CAVE MONSTERS

A secret underground atom testing laboratory in the town of Derby is sabotaged. Dr.WHO is dispatched to investigate and find the saboteurs to be intelligent lizard monsters from the past who plan to invade the Midlands town in collu... ...traitorous leader of the loca... ...ret communist agi... ...time to pre... th... d...

The Mysterious Dr. WHO and his Amazing Time-Automobile ready for more thrills

DR.WHO is the property of the British Broadcasting ... service of the United Kingdo...

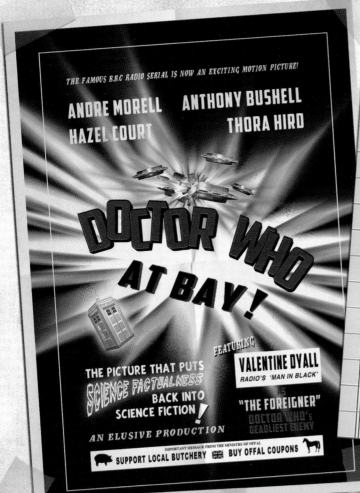

FUN AND THRILLS FROM BEYOND OUTER SPACE!!!

UNIVERSAL PICTURES Present An EXCLUSIVE FILMS Production

BUD ABBOTT & LOU COSTELLO MEET QUATERMASS

IN 3-DIMENSION

WHAT ON EARTH HAVE THE BOYS BROUGHT BACK FROM SPACE???

STARRING BRIAN DONLEVY

UNIVERSAL PICTURES Present An EXCLUSIVE FILMS Production
BUD ABBOTT & LOU COSTELLO in ABBOTT & COSTELLO MEET QUATERMASS
starring BRIAN DONLEVY   BARBARA SHELLEY   SIDNEY JAMES   JACK WARNER
and MICHAEL RIPPER Screenplay by NIGEL KNEALE and NORMAN HUDIS
Produced by MICHAEL CARRERAS Directed by VAL GUEST

ABBOTT & COSTELLO MEET QUATERMASS (1956)
Following the success of the first two Quatermass movies, Exclusive Films (later Hammer) wanted a third but noting the earlier success of Abbott & Costello Meet Frankenstein nearly a decade previous (and the fact that the two comedians were in the UK on a tour), it was suggested that a new direction might be a good idea. Nigel Kneale disagreed.

OLD MOTHER RILEY AND THE VENGEANCE OF CTHULHU

AS THE STENCH OF IMMORTAL EVIL DRIBBLES FROM THE FESTERING CORPSE OF ENGLAND, ONLY ONE WOMAN CAN SAVE THE COUNTRY FROM DOOM!!

ARTHUR LUCAN   KITTY McSHANE   DORA BRYAN   RICHARD WATTIS
and introducing little IAN McSHANE as YOUNG MOTHER RILEY

Screenplay by H. P. LOVECRAFT & VAL GUEST (Mr.)
Produced and Directed by ARTHUR P. CRAB-PASTE

A REWOUND PICTURES PICTURE

Filmed on location and at NETTLE RASH STUDIOS in GREAT ENGLAND
Distributed in the United States of Americans by carrier pigeons

"A NEW DIRECTION FOR OLD MOTHER RILEY... ONE THAT SHE CAN
KEEP GOING IN FOR ALL I CARE!"

NEW YORK DAILY NEWS

OLD MOTHER RILEY AND THE VENGEANCE OF CTHULHU (1954)
It's not widely known that Arthur Lucan was a white witch and under his witch name 'Azzula of the Oak' published a number of pamphlets and papers concerning the dark arts. He snapped up the chance to do a full-on super-natural film in the guise of Old Mother Riley and even managed to cast a dark spell that enabled his estranged wife Kitty McShane to appear in the film - allegedly of her own free will.

SOMEWHERE IN THE UNIVERSE THERE MUST BE SOMETHING BETTER THAN GEORGE?

IN THE MATTER OF A LUNCH - BREAK, A HUMBLE LANCASHIRE HANDY MAN WILL TUMBLE THROUGH THE CENTURIES AND FIND THE MOST WACKY ANSWER ON A STRANGE PLANET WHERE APES RULE AND MAN IS JUST PLAIN STUPID!

An unusual
and important
motion picture
from the
screenwriters of
"Let George
Do it!"

ELUSIVE FILMS present

GEORGE FORMBY ON THE
PLANET OF THE APES

Colour by Delux

STARRING
JAMES ROBERTSON-JUSTICE   THORA HIRD   HARRY FOWLER   ANTHONY BUSHELL   AND GUEST STARRING   BELA LUGOSI AS GENERAL BURKO

MUSIC BY ALBERT PICKLESTON   PRODUCED BY DONALD CONTRARY-SMITH   SCREENPLAY BY NELLIE ARTHRITIS & KEN COCK   FROM THE BOOK BY ENID BLYTON   DIRECTED BY PRU COPSTICK

GEORGE FORMBY ON THE PLANET OF
THE APES (1960)
Shortly before his death in 1961, there
were plans for a George Formby film –
his first one in over a decade. It was
written and cast but never made, possibly
because it would've proved too expensive
to make on a traditional Formby budget or
it could've been that 20th Century Fox
felt it was unsuitable for an ageing
Lancashire comedian and had bigger
plans for the script.

TELEVISION'S DARKEST HOUR BECOMES HOLLYWOOD'S MOST FRIGHTENING ENCOUNTER

Chosen...singled out for
humiliation...victim of
his imagination or
victim of a demon?

COLUMBIA PICTURES present

ROD HULL
MICHAEL PARKINSON

Night of the Emu

Screenplay by TALBOT ROTHWELL
Based on the Story "Casting the Loons" by M. R. STAINS
Directed by JACK TOURNIQUET

Executive Producer HAL E. BERRY

An EMU's BROADCASTING COMPANY Production

BBC tv

"More terrifying for my client
than GHOSTWATCH!"

MICHAEL PARKINSON'S AGENT

NIGHT OF THE EMU (1980)
PLEASE NOTE: This poster is cursed and
spells a disturbing death sentence for
all who gaze upon its countenance.

PLEASE DO NOT EXHIBIT.

Radio Times (Incorporating World-Radio)

NOVEMBER 23 - 29

Radio Times

SIXPENCE IN OLD MONEY

LONDON AND SOUTH-EAST

BBC
tv
Sound

DR. WHO

Eileen Way stars in a new Saturday teatime drama series for all the family. She portrays a cave woman who doesn't want her tribe to regain the secret of fire and will stop at nothing to prevent it.

SEE PAGE 13

BEYOND OUR KEN

Kenneth Horne returns in a new radio comedy series which is sort-of funny.

SEE PAGE 7

JFK ASSASSINATION!

Live coverage from Dallas and the United States continues from Friday.

SEE PAGE 26

SOVIET STATE CIRCUS

Join comrade ringmasters Nikita Khrushchev and Leonid Brezhnev in the big red top located on a field just outside Moscow for thrills, spills and tractors.

SEE PAGE 27

THE LOST WORLD OF
Dr WHO's TIME TEAM

ROBERT MORLEY   JIMMY CLITHEROE   NORMAN BATES

DOCTOR WHO TIME TEAM

DOCTO
W

by Sherry-Lee Bentham

The story of BBC3 goes back to the early sixties. In 1961, it was decided via a number of high level committee meetings, that the BBC would need a third channel by the year 2003. BBC2 was already in the pipeline and had been since the forties when Lord Reith himself rubber-stamped the idea. It was set to debut on schedule in a few years time once the colour of the announcer's desk had been finally decided.* The actual feasibility of BBC3 would need to be rigorously tested in the mean time. This would be done by secretly establishing a small television station in South Devon and measuring viewer response to its test programming. One of the first ideas for shows was something to accompany the corporation's new science fiction serial 'Dr WHO' as a way of determining whether viewers would switch over to watch additional content about a show they had just watched. Thus the 'Dr WHO Time Team' was created. Presented by Katie Boyle and featuring a selection of special guests, each edition featured lively

discussions about the latest episode as well as Robert Robinson reading out viewers' letters concerning the previous week's episode (mostly from a Mrs Collins in Dawlish) There were also star interviews and some behind the scenes features where things like inlay and ring modulators were explained. It was all broadcast live at 7pm. Sadly, very little remains in the BBC Archives save for a handful of photographs, a 'Programme-As-Broadcast' (PASB) document for an early edition and a brief mention in the Radio Times where the listing writer refers to it as 'The Dr WHO Fan Show' - an early working title that would be re-used decades later for a rebooted version aimed at young people of a certain age. An attempt was made to chronicle the show in a book but the author could only be arsed to put together two pages of an episode guide before succumbing to money and a contract to put together a forty volume history of ATV's 'Crossroads' which would eventually be published in Austria where they still carry the series. The surviving documents are reproduced on the following pages.

* It was a teak desk with non-glare varnish

Katie Boyle was the host for the entire seven year run of 'Dr. Who's Time Team. She's seen here sat on the double bed that she used for a brief time when budget issues meant that the programme had to be recorded after 1am in the morning. It was found in storage decades later and was auctioned for charity at the BBC's twentieth anniversary event at Longleat House in 1983. The successul bidder was Brian Blessed.

One of the most popular features of the series was the annual season poll where viewers voted for their favourite story once the production team had decided what to call each one. Here's Dodo actress JACKIE LANE casting a generous vote for 'The Temple of Secrets', little realising that she wasn't actually in it.

A work-to-rule by scene shifters meant that the TARDIS prop wasn't removed from the studio when it was used for live coverage of the 1966 World Cup of Foot Ball. David Coleman was very angry as he was not a fan of Dr WHO and forbade his children to watch it as he considered it too frightening. He let rip at a meeting the following day which resulted in the the spilling of blood according to official accident reports from the time.

Ms Boyle managed to secure a rare interview with the normally shy WILLIAM HARTNELL. The actor appeared quite jovial during the twenty minute chat but witnesses say he was quite edgy whilst having his wig applied. Hartnell was paid an additional two guineas to wear his Dr Who costume though he was allowed to wear carpet slippers due to his persistant corns.

A celebrity team consisting of LADY ISOBEL BARNETT, MACDONALD HOBLEY, LUCILLE BALL and SYDNEY NEWMAN were invited onto the show to guess the differences between a television Dalek and one from the then new movie DALEKS INVASION EARTH 2150AD. They managed forty-seven and went forward to represent the UK at the Eurovision Dr Who Brain of Europe 1967 in Stockholm.

Dr WHO Time Team - episode guide - series A

Episode one (The Dead Planet)

Presenter:	**Katie Boyle**	**Expert guest:**	**Patrick Moore**
Desk presenter:	**Robert Robinson**	**Monologue:**	**Cy Grant**
Panel:	**Jimmy Edwards**		
	Jimmy Clitheroe		
	Susan Hampshire		
	Edgar Lustgarten		

The panel discussed the first episode to be written by Terry Nation. Film clip shown of Dr WHO and his fellow travellers exiting time machine. Ms. Boyle discussed the absurdity of life on other planets with astronomer Patrick Moore. Robert Robinson read out viewers letters about how awful the caveman story from the previous week was. Susan Hampshire said she was looking forward to seeing what was on the end of the rubber plunger. She hoped it was not an angry plumber!

Notes: *Katie Boyle introduced the show wearing a satin evening dress booked from BBC Wardrobe on the previous Tuesday at 4.18pm. The lengthy lead time was to allow it to be painted lime green in order to prevent it from flaring on the TV cameras.*

Jimmy Clitheroe was a last minute addition to the panel at the request of Sydney Newman who was keen that there should be some representation of the target audience on the programme

Cy Grant sang a calypso over the end credits about getting lost in a forest made of stone.

Edgar Lustgarten performed some of ther voices for the viewers' letters. In future episodes, the voices would be done by Peter Hawkins and Leila Williams depending on their sex.

Recorded at Lime Grove: 20.12.1964
TX: 6.15om - 22.12.1964

Episode two (The Survivors)

Presenter:	**Katie Boyle**	**Expert guest:**	**David Attenborough**
Desk presenter:	**Robert Robinson**	**Monologue:**	**Terry-Thomas**
Panel:	**David Nixon**		
	Barbara Kelly		
	Sid Green		
	Freddie Garrity		

The panel discussed the second episode of the new serial and in particular, the Dalek robot people. Sid Green made a joke about Dalek gender being salt and pepper that Barbara Kelly thought was tasteless so Sid suggested she puts some vinegar on it as well. Ms Boyle talked to David Attenborough about mutations and he showed her a snake. Robert Robinson apologised to viewers for all the bed-wetting that had ocurred following the previous week's Dr WHO cliffhanger. Freddie Garrity sung his new music record to a pair of Daleks in the studio. Terry-Thomas related an anecdote about fish.

Notes: *Katie Boyle was late into the studio by ten minutes due to a hair appointment and plans were put in place to replace her with Leila Williams who'd popped into the building to drop off her ID card two years too late.*

Sid Green replaced Frankie Howerd at the suggestion of Sydney Newman as the drama chief hated Howerd's "bloody guts!".

The end credits mispelled Robert Robinson's name as "Robertson" and the presenter was paid £2 10s 7d as compensation.

Recorded at Lime Grove: 20.12.1964
TX: 6.16pm - 29.12.1964

Episode three (The Escape)

Presenter: Katie Boyle

Desk presenter: Kenneth Kendall

Panel: Eamonn Andrews
Terrence Longdon
Betty Marsden
Harry Corbett & Sooty

Expert guest: George Cansdale

Monologue: William Rushton

The programme began with the panel talking about the previous night's episode with Betty Marsden commenting on the Thal fashions and how she would like to get her sewing kit on the Thal men's trousers. Sooty didn't mention the episode much but baked Betty a magic cake. George Cansdale showed Ms Boyle how radiation can break down the structure of biological matter whilst Kenneth Kendall read a selection of the viewer's letters. Of particular mention was one from eight year old Alison Bennett of Great Yarmouth who observed that the Thals looked a bit "milquetoast". William Rushton did a monolgue about the last magnadon on Skaro.

Notes: *Sooty very nearly didn't appear as Harry Corbett arrived at the studio to find he had accidentally packed two Sweep puppets in his suitcase for the journey down from Yorkshire. A prop man had to nip out and purchase a Sooty puppet from Hamleys for the sum of five shillings.*

The studio recording was attended by Katie Boyle's youngest son Frankie.

Kenneth Kendall replaced Robert Robinson by arrangement with the latter's agent after it was found his appearance clashed with a motorway services opening ceremony that had been booked over a month previous. Kendall was paid £20 for his services and allowed to keep the suit.

The magnadon prop was the same one used in the Dr WHO serial. It was damaged when Betty Marsden accidentally sat on it and had to be destroyed whilst the prop was returned to the Dr WHO production office.

Recorded at Lime Grove: 3.1.1964
TX: 6.15pm - 5.1.1964

Episode three (The Ambush)

Presenter: Katie Boyle

Desk presenter: Robert Robinson

Panel: Lady Isobel Barnet
Freddie Trueman
Andrew Cruickshank
Alan Freeman
The Television Toppers

Expert guest: Professor Stanley Unwin

Monologue: Kenneth Williams

After a surprisingly short discussion about the previous night's episode, Ms Boyle spent the next five minutes in conversation with Stanley Unwin in a pre-filmed sequence that involved the famous orator arriving in the Police Box time ship. Kenneth Williams read a specially written poem about the Daleks with illustrations by Tony Hart. Following a quick chat with Alan Freeman about his love of science fiction (and a brief mention of the following week's Top of the Pops), The Television Toppers performed a dance routine to the instrumental Telstar... and were joined by a Dalek as the end credits rolled.

Notes: *The shortness of the panel discussion was the result of an argument that occurred during the recording between Cruickshank and Trueman. Both disagreed on the effectiveness of Tristram Cary's musique concrete on the Dr WHO episode with Trueman threatening to lamp the elderly Scottish actor when he suggested that the cricketer's cat on heat could create better music.*

Alan Freeman's appearance was at the request of BBC Programme Publicity as the disc jockey was due to present the second edition of the new Top of the Pops show which had started that week. Jimmy Savile was unavailable.

The Television Toppers performed their dance routine dressed in the female Thal costumes which had to be rushed to the studio following their use in the final episode of the Dalek Dr WHO serial.

From 12.45

GRANDSTAND

featuring

COCK FIGHTING . . .

FOX HUNTING . . .

BUDGIE HARRASSING . . .

as well as

HEARSE RACING
from BRAY

2.0 **Count Yorga's Hurdle race (Div. II)**
(over 34 miles)

2.30 **Van Helsing's Stakes**
(over 1 mile, 3 Edward Furlongs)

3.0 **Chase Blacula Chase**
(over before it's started)

4.0 **Injured Horse Shooting Live**
(depends on numbers really)

Commentators: **Peter Cushing**
and **Christopher Lee**

Television presentation by Dennis Satan

KANGAROO BOXING
from Melbourne, Derbyshire

WILFRED HYDE WHITE
v.
DANNY THE ROO
Commentator: **Peter Glaze**

MOTORING ROADKILL
from Smethwick

THE MISS TIGGYWINKLE
MEMORIAL TROPHY

Commentator: **Murray Walker**
and The Television Vet

PIANIST FIGHT OF THE WEEK
Winnifred Atwell v.
Liberace

Filmed highlights of this week's top-of-
-the-bill bout at the Tipton Working Men's
Club.

Commentator: **Jimmy Tarbuck**

Followed by

Full Results Service
This week read by special guests
Harry Corbett & Sooty

Live from London (If wet, Basingstoke)

9.25

GARDENING CLUB

*A film visit to a small courtyard garden in
Chiswick for a special session of clubbing.*

Percy Thrower
with
Frankie Howerd
Eamonn Andrews
and
Edwin Richfield

Title music by RON GRAINER
and arranged by SEGUN AKINOLA
Producer, NIKKI WILSON
Executive Producers, CHRIS CHIBNALL
                                    & MATT STREVENS
Directed by JAMIE CHILDS

9.55

LET'S BUILD A COFFIN

*A comprehensive guide on how to construct
something that we will all need eventually;
for the noted expert or the talented novice.*

Barry Bucknall

is joined by members of the Chiswick Car-
pentary Society for today's lesson which
is the sixth in this educational series.

Title music by GUSTAV HOLST
Produced by MARY FONT

10.15

HEY, IT'S ESPERANTO!

*Learn the popular new language that will
eventually replace every language in the
world.*

Mary Malcolm

is your guide along with leading expert
Dr Edna Panopoly

Lesson Twenty-seven: In which you are
introduced to the basics of sentence
mutation and the fundamental core establishment of variable conjugation with an
emphasis on what to do in relationship sit-
uations with pets and other domesticated
animals.

Written by ALISTAIR PENTAGRAM
Produced by CARLOS FEAR

10.40

PEOPLE EATING
FOREIGN FOOD

Introduced by
David Nixon

This week: Italian Spaghetti

Produced by THE BBC CANTEEN FILM UNIT

followed by

INTERLUDE

12.45PM

GRANDSTAND

See panel left

5.15

TOM AND JERRY

A cartoon film short presentation
starring **TOM THE CAT** and a far-from-
underdog mouse called **JERRY**.

in

"The Yankee Doodle Mouse"

In this exciting *Award Winning* installment
from the popular cartoon series, Tom
pursues Jerry through a cellar, but the
mouse successfully dives into his mouse-
hole. Tom peers into the hole, and Jerry
launches a tomato from a mousetrap into
his face. Jerry then climbs up the wall and
grabs a handful of eggs from a carton
marked *"Hen-Grenades"*. As Tom wipes
the tomato off his face, he is promptly
covered in egg, with one hit to the eye
leaving the effect of him wearing a
monocle. Jerry shoots off the corks from a
champagne case, knocking Tom into a tub
of water with only a pot to keep him afloat.
The mouse promptly launches a brick from
a spatula, sinking both the pot and Tom.
Leading to the 1st war communiqué
message, it reads *"Sighted cat – sank same.
Signed, Lt. Jerry Mouse"*. Meanwhile...

Created by WILLIAM HANNA
and JOE BARBARA
Producer, FRED QUIMBY
Music by SCOTT BRADLEY
Directed by WILLIAM HANNA
and JOE BARBARA
Layouts by HARVEY EISENBERG
Animation by IRVEN SPENCE,
PETE BURNESS, KENNETH MUSE,
GEORGE GORDON and
JACK ZANDER
An M.G.M. Release

5.25

DR. WHO

Outer space thrills.

Produced by VERITY LAMBERT

INFORMATION FOR VIEWERS IN DEVON
*Remember if you live in Dawlish and parts
of the surrounding South Devon you may
be able to tune your television receiver to
BBC television's experimental BBC3
broadcasts as 'The Dr. Who Fan Show'
will air after a short interlude film at 6.0.*

5.45

THE NEWS

6.0

JUKE BOX JURY

A new disc - is it a HIT or a MISS?

Comment and opinions on
the latest pop releases.

This week's panel is:

Brian Donlevy
John Profumo
Jimmy Clitheroe
Esma Cannon
In the chair: **David Jacobs**
On the ceiling: **Keith Moon**

Programme devised by COCO THE CHIMP
Produced by BANDIGROVE SHADRACK

TELEVISION SERVICE: SUNDAY: Continued 2

18.15.01 VT DR. WHO'S TIME TEAM: EPISODE 1
(Telerecorded on closed circuit 20.12.1963 - VT/T/30665
Produced by Montgomery Butcher (20'21")
Studio Director: James Coonte

Cast:-
Presenter________________Katie Boyle
Taking part:
Jimmy Clitheroe
Jimmy Edwards
Edgar Lustgarten
Susan Hampshire
and
a member of the public (unknown)

FILM SEQUENCES USED
Footage: 2'35" Sound 35mm

MUSIC ON FILM
Ron Grainer and ensemble
Opening Music
00'20" Ron Grainer
(With John Barry Combo
and Radiophonic effects from BBC sound library)

RECORDS DUBBED:
Laughing Policeman (Arthur Askey) 1a 665B
Gratuitous Raspberry Sound Effect (BBC RW) 2a 772C
Smack My Bitch Up (The Prodigy) 2c 295V

18.36.32 SYMBOL/IDENT

18.37.00 INTERLUDE

"KITTENS PLAYING NEAR COMBINE HARVESTER"
35mm - Telecine

MUSIC ON FILM
MARS THE BRINGER OF WAR (Gustav Holst)
Norrie Paraglide and the Northern Comb & Paper Ensemble

NB Sorry about the smell. I had to do this on the school photocopier.

BBC tv

THE DOCTOR WHO

6ᵈ

GARDEN FETE
ONE YEAR OF A TIME TRAVELLER

COMM...
PRO...

The BBC Exploitation Department presents

The Dr. Who Garden Fete
One Year of a Time Traveller

The Vicarage Garden Mayfield, Sussex
(if wet, church hall)

Sunday, 30th, August, 1964 10.30AM until 5.00PM

ADMIT ONE SENIOR CITIZEN 2/6ᵈ

Does not include toilet access

One Day Only Ticket

№ 0003

№ 0003

...presents

...presents

ADMIT...

Sunday...

...Only Ticket

AS/20/P

From: Verity Lambert - Prod. "DR.WHO"

Subject: "DR.WHO PUBLIC CELEBRATION EVENT"   BY HAND

To: Sydney Newman - H.S.S. Tel   14th July 1964

Dear Sydney,

I think having a public celebration of our first year is a
splendid idea. However, things may have developed far quicker
and in ways you couldn't have forseen.
I mentioned it to Bill in passing and he agreed to it in principle
but wanted to check with Heather first. Now I'm not sure what
he said to her or whether he misunderstood me but it appears that
he has booked his local vicarage and church hall believing I
wanted a garden fete as a celebration. He's come back to me full
of ideas and has also got Carole, Jackie and Russ to help out.

At the moment, Jackie is supplying cakes for a cake stall and
has got the support of some of her Women's Institute friends to
sort out homemade jams and potted seedlings. Carole has said she
wants to do a coconut shy but has no idea where to get them.
And (surprise, surprise!), Bill and Russ are volunteering to run
the beer tent. Yesterday evening, Mervyn popped his head round
the door with one of those electric buzzing wire toys that he'd
made his kids last year. He says
we can have it for a stall.

I think it all might be getting a bit out of hand as I now have
Delia and Brian at the Workshop saying they can get hold of
some acts if we want live music.

If we do this, I hope we can expect around 100 to 150 attendees;
mostly from the locale. I don't forsee a huge crowd as knowing
the British weather, it will all get rained off anyway.

What do you think?

(Verity Lambert)

AN OFFICIAL BRITISH BROADCASTING CORPORATION MEMORANDUM

From: Peter Pronderghast   Suite 4B   Broadcasting House

Subject: Verbiage for Doctor Who open air recreational   BY HAND

To: Verity Lambert   Producer - Doctor Who   30th July 1964

My dearest Ms Verity Lambert,

Please find enclosed the verbiage we have put together for the announcement of your Doctor Who open air recreational which we will read to viewers following the closing caption of Prisoners of Conciegerie; this being the final programme in your first sequence of episodic presentations. I have spoken with Gimlet Pronderghast who will be the speaking announcer that evening and he will contact you shortly regarding his attire for the speech. He normally goes formal after the football result but may wish to loosen his tie given the recreational nature of your event.

Here are the words.

"If you enjoy viewing the weekly adventures of Doctor Who, then you might want to be aware that the BBC is planning a celebratory garden fete style event in the village of Mayfield later this year. Tickets and information are available from the BBC at this address. (INSERT ADDRESS HERE.) Please do remember to included a stamped self-addressed envelope for a reply. And now back to our normal programmes for the evening as David Jacobs chairs another edition of the Juke Box Jury."

Peter.

Nothing to be written or typed in this margin

Nothing to be written or typed in this box.

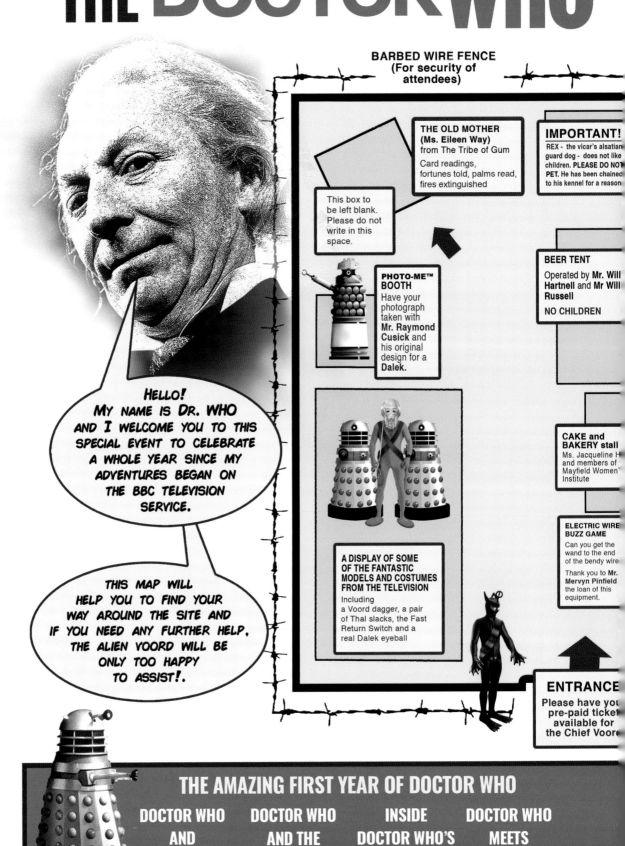

CELEBRATION FETE 1964

THE VICARAGE GARDEN, MAYFIELD
SUNDAY 30th AUGUST 1964

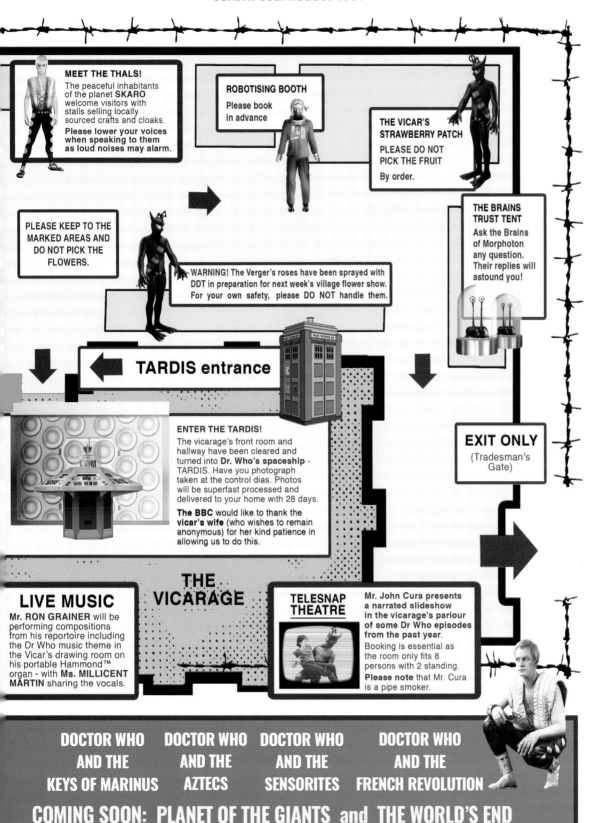

MEET THE THALS!
The peaceful inhabitants of the planet **SKARO** welcome visitors with stalls selling locally sourced crafts and cloaks.

Please lower your voices when speaking to them as loud noises may alarm.

ROBOTISING BOOTH
Please book in advance

THE VICAR'S STRAWBERRY PATCH
PLEASE DO NOT PICK THE FRUIT
By order.

PLEASE KEEP TO THE MARKED AREAS AND DO NOT PICK THE FLOWERS.

THE BRAINS TRUST TENT
Ask the Brains of Morphoton any question. Their replies will astound you!

WARNING! The Verger's roses have been sprayed with DDT in preparation for next week's village flower show. For your own safety, please DO NOT handle them.

TARDIS entrance

ENTER THE TARDIS!
The vicarage's front room and hallway have been cleared and turned into **Dr. Who's spaceship** - TARDIS. Have you photograph taken at the control dias. Photos will be superfast processed and delivered to your home with 28 days.

The BBC would like to thank the **vicar's wife** (who wishes to remain anonymous) for her kind patience in allowing us to do this.

EXIT ONLY
(Tradesman's Gate)

THE VICARAGE

LIVE MUSIC
Mr. RON GRAINER will be performing compositions from his reportoire including the Dr Who music theme in the Vicar's drawing room on his portable Hammond™ organ - with **Ms. MILLICENT MARTIN** sharing the vocals.

TELESNAP THEATRE

Mr. John Cura presents a narrated slideshow in the vicarage's parlour of some Dr Who episodes from the past year.
Booking is essential as the room only fits 8 persons with 2 standing.
Please note that Mr. Cura is a pipe smoker.

DOCTOR WHO AND THE KEYS OF MARINUS　　**DOCTOR WHO AND THE AZTECS**　　**DOCTOR WHO AND THE SENSORITES**　　**DOCTOR WHO AND THE FRENCH REVOLUTION**

COMING SOON: PLANET OF THE GIANTS and THE WORLD'S END

OR CITIZEN 2/6
Does not include toilet access

0:30AM until 5.00pm

E R
LONDON N.C.

ALICE GORMANGHAST
Road,

INCORPORATED PRESS ASSOCIATION PHOTOGRAPH: Date: XX XX XXXX

DESCRIPTION: Things at a garden fete to celebrate the BBC televisual serial Dr. Who got out
of hand when a Police Box was found not to be the one used in the actual BBC production.
Pictured from left to right: Mr. Arthur Plank (Behind), Mr. Henry Valhala, Mr. Ernie Cramp
and Mr. Dennis Toucan.   Rights released.   Photo: ©1964 IPA Pictorial.

The BBC Exploitation Department presents
The Dr. Who Garden Fete
One Year of a Time

Sunday

№ 0003

HAVE
YOUR
PHOTOGRAPH
TAKEN WITH
THE
ORIGINAL
DR WHO
TARDIS
POLICE BOX

Daily Mirror

3d. Monday, September 1, 1964

Sussex traffic MISERY

Dr. WHO's BANK HOLIDAY CHAOS

A Sussex garden fete to celebrate the first year of BBCtv's latest children's serial Dr. WHO caused a huge traffic jam that affected most of Sussex and the surrounding area yesterday.

The celebratory event which featured appearances by the stars of the Saturday night BBCtv serial was planned as a small local affair but word got out to the rest of the country resulting in tens of thousands of eager television viewers blocking roads into and out of the county.

STUCK

Organisers which included the programme's BBC producer Verity Lambert said they could not have forseen the popularity. *"The first that we knew about it was when one of our team became stuck in traffic and had to call the vicarage by telephone. Funnily enough, he used one of the few remaining police boxes in the area to do so!"* She laughed.

Actor Hartnell: *beer tent*

SICK

Not laughing was Mrs N Capaldi who along with her young son, Peter (6) had travelled all the way down from Glasgow to enable Peter to meet his hero, Dr Who. *"We managed to get a taxi from the nearest railway station but became stuck in traffic four miles outside Mayfield where the event was taking place. We ended up stuck in the jam for most of the day and didn't arrive at the gates until half an hour before the end of the fete. To make matters worse, little Peter got car sick and the taxi driver mades us pay for the drycleaning."* She also said that some of the stars of the television show had already left the site and that only star William Hartnell was there. *"He appeared to be asleep in the beer tent. Little Peter tried to say hello to but got short shrift from the vicar who was also trying to move the gentleman. It was horrible. I feel so sorry for my son who witnessed this whole sorry debacle. Heaven knows, what he will make of it in his later years. He idolised Mr Hartnell."* She added.

Producer Lambert: *Sorry*

Alien: *Voord*

SILENCE

We approached Mr Hartnell for a comment but his agent said he was *"...recovering from a heavy workload and was unable to come downstairs."*

Traffic backed up into neighbouring counties causing delays of up to 15hours.

Horoscopes Page 17 **Television** Page 24 **Pork Markets** Page 29

All hail...
Cleo-Cat-Barbara-tra

NEW

Hand-crafted by blind artisan bakers

Painted fully by a hand using a keyboard on a big machine

Gold bits that really flake off after a few weeks

Only **£39.99***

* Not actual price.

Actual figure more disturbing than that shown.

Everybody loves cats!

Everybody is fascinated by the Ancient Egyptians!

Everybody has the upmost respect for famed history teacher BARBARA WRIGHT from TV's Dr. WHO television programmes!

Now you can own your very own BARBARA WRIGHT - not just as a cat! AS AN ANCIENT EGYPTIAN CAT!!

Yes, all your dreams have come true as House of Hamilton-Dyce proudly releases this exclusive figurine just for you and all the other collectors of this sort of thing.

Based on the artwork of renowned pig breeder and convicted fraudster EMILY SPROUG, this exquisitely produced ornament is sure to look stunning wherever you choose to stick it.

And what's more... world-class electronics mean that her eyes light up when placed in the vicinity of a strong wi-fi signal! INCREDIBLE isn't it?

You'll love BARBARA WRIGHT even more if you choose to act now and fill in the simple coupon. Send it now and we will despatch your very own cardboard box in which will be this incredible work of art that you will want to hand down to your children immediately. Do it now. There's no time to lose. Get a pen and write your details in the box. You know you want to. DO IT!

Your Reservation Coupon Thing
Please respond promptly and as soon as possible now.

To. HOUSE OF HAMILTON-DYCE, Beckerly Insane Asylum, Wolfham, SOUTHSHIRE.

YES! Please reserve for me .... (Qty) of your hauntingly beautiful Cleo-Cat-Barbara-Tra figurine as vividly described in your well-written and engaging ad.

Name (Mr/Mrs/Miss/Ms/Brigadier)...

Address...

Postcode.. Telephone ....

Applicants must be old enough to know better. UK Mainland addresses only as we got caught by the FBI last time we sent one to the US. We may choose to contact you either by mail or email... just to put the wind up you.

"You CANNOT change this credit agreement. Not one line of it!!!"

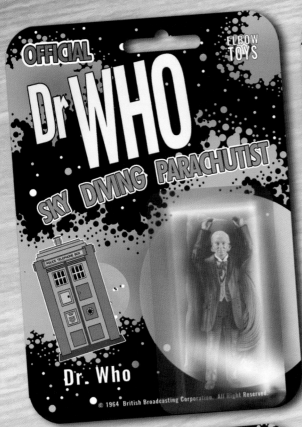

OFFICIAL

ELBOW TOYS

Dr WHO

SKY DIVING PARACHUTIST

POLICE TELEPHONE BOX

Dr. Who

© 1964 British Broadcasting Corporation. All Right Reserved

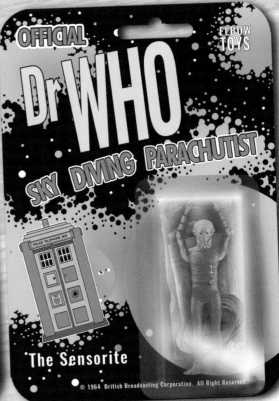

OFFICIAL

ELBOW TOYS

Dr WHO

SKY DIVING PARACHUTIST

POLICE TELEPHONE BOX

The Sensorite

© 1964 British Broadcasting Corporation. All Right Reserved

OFFICIAL

ELBOW TOYS

Dr WHO

SKY DIVING PARACHUTIST

POLICE TELEPHONE BOX

Robotman

...tion. All Right Reserved

OFFICIAL

ELBOW TOYS

Dr WHO

SKY DIVING PARACHUTIST

POLICE TELEPHONE BOX

Alien Voord

© 1964 British Broadcasting Corporation. All Right Reserved

Four Dr WHO Sky Diving Parachutist toys.

Produced by ELBOW TOYS in the mid-sixties

VERY RARE (These weren't available to the
general public but were produced to be used in
military excercises as target practice. One
featuring Barbara Wright was withdrawn due
to objections from the actress.)

THE DALOGRAPHY OF SKARO

Scale: 1 : 150 700.000 < 370 * to 1 space mile

Produced by Solarius Cartography for the Space Security Service (Bejing, Earth)

The Ocean of Sea

The Radox Mines of Paladium

The Sound of Breaking Glass

THE RIVER OF UNCOMFORTABLE WATERS

LIDL

The Serpent Sea

DAVIUS

The Bran Farran Supository

ALDI

Alydon's Knob

Russell

Forty Skardels off the coast of Davius is a mysterious zone of fresh water. It is home to thousands of giant aluminium serpents that have evolved due to the high metal content of the ocean bed. Efforts to map this area have failed due to the dangerous and unpredictable weather systems. Ice tornados and jelly tsunami can form from nowhere and many researchers have been lost over the decades. Legend has it that the aluminium serpents have dominion over the elements in this area...

The continent of DAVIUS is peopled by the Thals - a kindly race of tall, fair, handsome people with dreadful taste in fashion.

In the centuries following The Great Skaron War, the Thals mutated into hideous creatures but over time their physical deformities went full circle and they returned to their physically perfect humanoid form.

They also pledged an oath of pacifism and became farmers of the land. A burning drought in the space calendar year 43287 led them to seek help from their ancient enemies the Dals... but their efforts were in vain as the Dals too had evolved... but into vile agressive creatures still bent on their destruction.

The Ocean of Ooze

The Lake of Mutation

The Sea of Oceans

DEREK

The Lake of Mutations is open daily throughout the summer from 7am until 9pm every day except bank holidays. Visitors are asked to wear suitable clothing and not to bathe in the waters unarmed. Free car parking on weekdays.

THE FORBIDDEN ISLANDS

The Ocean of Ooze, like so much of Skaro, is still a mystery. Apparently, a vast swathe of the inner sea is composed of ooze. Yes, ooze. This makes the water impossible to navigate by conventional means. It's not thick enough to walk on and not thin enough to sail a boat through. It's a bloody mess and smells a bit off. Kids will love it.

The Lake of Turpentine

Davros' Beach Property

The Forbidden Islands are so called as they are forbidden. Explorers have attempted to chart these mysterious isles but as they approached the coastlines, they were forbidden to go any further. The reason for the islands' isolation is a secret known only to the Dalek Emperor... and he is forbidden to discuss them. This label is also forbidden and will shortly be removed.

DALAZAR - Continent of the Daleks. This is the most habitable part of Skaro - a mixture of arid radio active deserts and petrified jungles.

The Dalek city is built on a former undergound radiation shelter where the Daleks' original forms - the Dals - hid in the closing decades of the Great Skaron War. With the defences falling and the Dals mutating in the neutronic radiation, the Daleks were born - mobile survival pods for their mutant genetic form.

When the Daleks emerged, it was as a powerful war-like race with a hatred for all that was different to them. For centuries, they remained within their city powered by electro-static floors until the discovery and realisation they were not alone in the universe when a Time Lord and his allies from across the stars all but destroyed the survivors...

It was then that they began plotting the galaxy's subjugation.

NORTH TARRANT

The
Topless
Mountains

DAGENHAM

The Caves of
Glass Fibres

The
Bottomless
Sea

Tomb of the
Unknown
Roboman

The Bottomless Sea is neither bottomless nor a sea. The exact origins of its name are lost to time.

A range of mountains formed entirely of bakelite. It was here that the Daleks originally mined the molten radio active salt that powered their city before they discovered that static electricity was both safer and less hazardous.

DARREN

The
Radiation
Range

The
Cosmic
Ray Aga

The
Neutonic
Stove

The Sea of Acid

DALEK
CITY

The
Bay
of
No
Shame

Marinian
Embassy

TOILETS

DALAZAR

DERVLA

Kirwan

Mechon
Labour
Camp

The
Sea of
Rust

DANONE

SOUTH TARRANT

The chemical polution from the Great Skaron War resulted in the formation of The Sea of Rust - an area of ocean where anything remaining in it for more than a few minutes, turns to rust... even living beings. Despite reports to the contrary, the water doesn't taste of Irn Bru.

The Island of
Gushing Yoghurt

6ᵈ

No. 4 November 23 1963 Saturdays

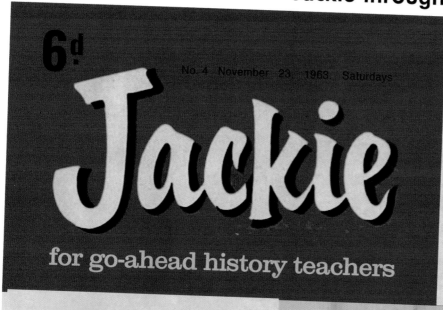

Jackie

for go-ahead history teachers

BARBARA UNLIMITED

colour colour colour

colour colour

pin ups

colour colour colour

the AZTECS | the ZARBI

THE ALIEN VOORD

GEORGE COULOURIS

stereo

PARLOPHONE EMI

MATT MONRO
sings THE RESCUE

Music & Songs inspired by the
popular "Dr. WHO" serial

MATT MONRO sings THE RESCUE

SIDE ONE:

1. From Dido With Love (Black/Barry)

2. You Can't Come In! (Black/Barry)

3. Space Capsule (Barry)

4. Koquillion! (Black/Barry)

5. Bennett's Lament (Black/Barry)

SIDE TWO:

1. Oh, Sandy! (Black/Barry)

2. Didodian Requiem (Barry)

3. Dr. Who's Oompa Music (Barry)

4. I Had a Little Sandbeast (Black/Barry)

5. Welcome Aboard, Vicki! (Black/Barry)

Based on the BBCtv serial Dr Who and the Rescue
Original screenplay by David Whitaker
Album produced by George Martin

Recorded at ABBEY ROAD
STUDIOS, ENGLAND

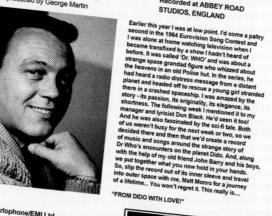

Earlier this year I was at low point. I'd come a paltry second in the 1964 Eurovision Song Contest and I was alone at home watching television when I became transfixed by a show I hadn't heard of before. It was called 'Dr. WHO' and was about a strange space grandad figure who whizzed about the heavens in an old Police hut. In the series, he had heard a radio distress message from a distant planet and headed off to rescue a young girl stranded there in a crashed spaceship. I was amazed by the story - its passion, its originality, its elegance, its shortness. The following week I mentioned it to my manager and lyricist Don Black. He'd seen it too! And he was also fascinated by the sci-fi tale. Both of us weren't busy for the next week or two, so we decided there and then that we'd create a record of music and songs around the strange story of Dr Who's encounters on the planet Dido. And, along with the help of my old friend John Barry and his boys, we put together what you now hold in your hands. So, slip the record out of its inner sleeve and travel into outer space with me, Matt Monro for a journey of a lifetime... You won't regret it. This really is....

"FROM DIDO WITH LOVE!"

(P) 1965 Parlophone/EMI Ltd

PARLOPHONE EMI

SOUNDS LIKE A CLASSIC

Garrod

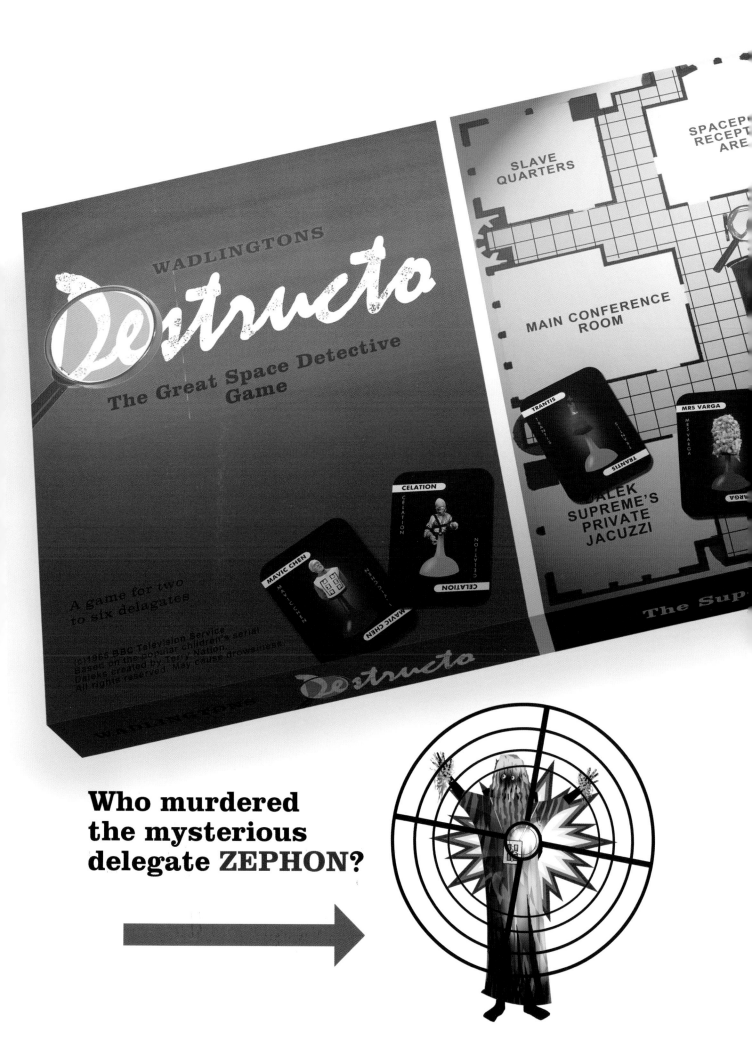

WADLINGTONS

Destructo

The Great Space Detective Game

A game for two to six delegates

Destructo

WADLINGTONS

SLAVE QUARTERS

SPACEP... RECEPT... ARE...

MAIN CONFERENCE ROOM

TRANTIS

MRS VARGA

DALEK SUPREME'S PRIVATE JACUZZI

CELATION

MAVIC CHEN

The Sup...

Who murdered the mysterious delegate ZEPHON?

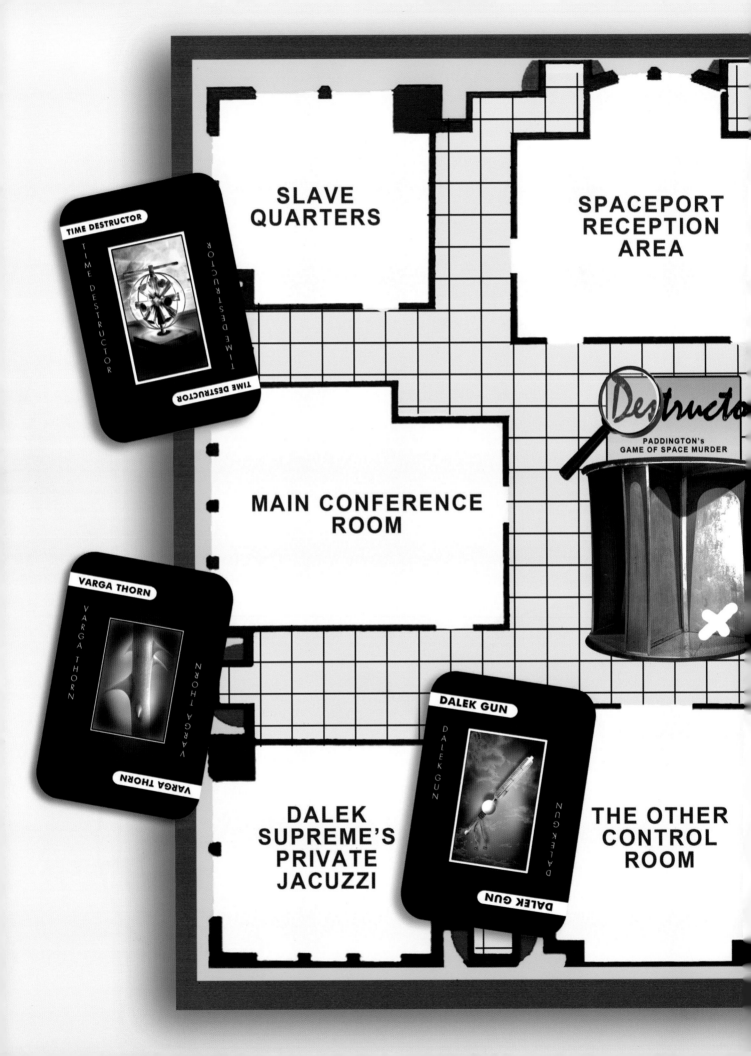

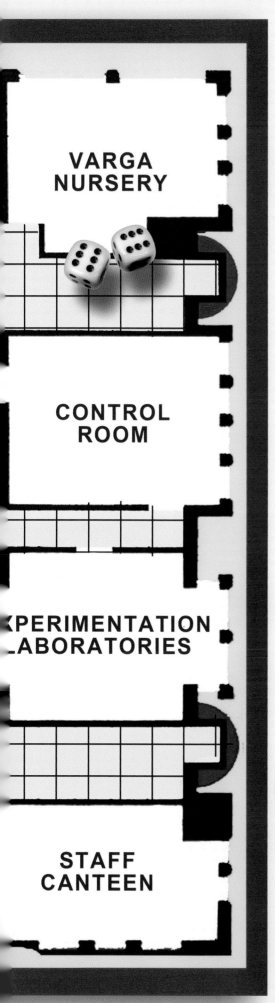

VARGA
NURSERY

CONTROL
ROOM

XPERIMENTATION
ABORATORIES

STAFF
CANTEEN

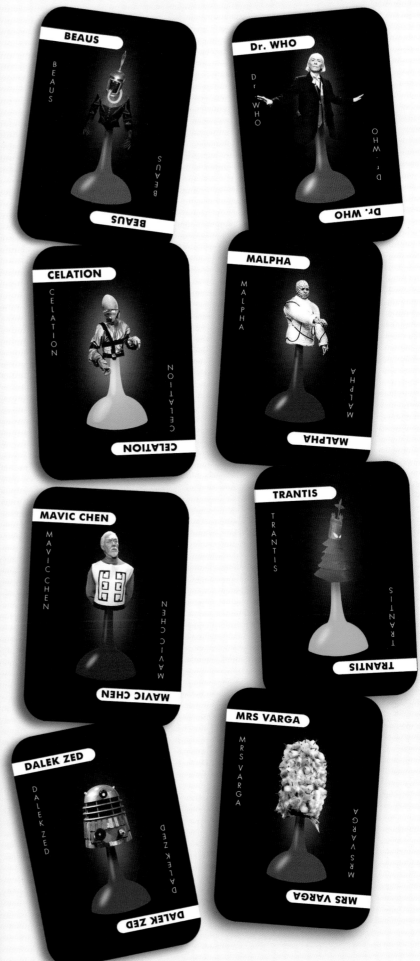

BEAUS

Dr. WHO

CELATION

MALPHA

MAVIC CHEN

TRANTIS

DALEK ZED

MRS VARGA

SPAR

Terran spin-drive presidential space yacht

Owners Workshop Manual

step-by-step maintenance and repair

Straynes ®

...ace yacht manuals in

MAVIC CHEN'S SPACESHIP - ABANDONED AT BROMLEY STATION

2A86

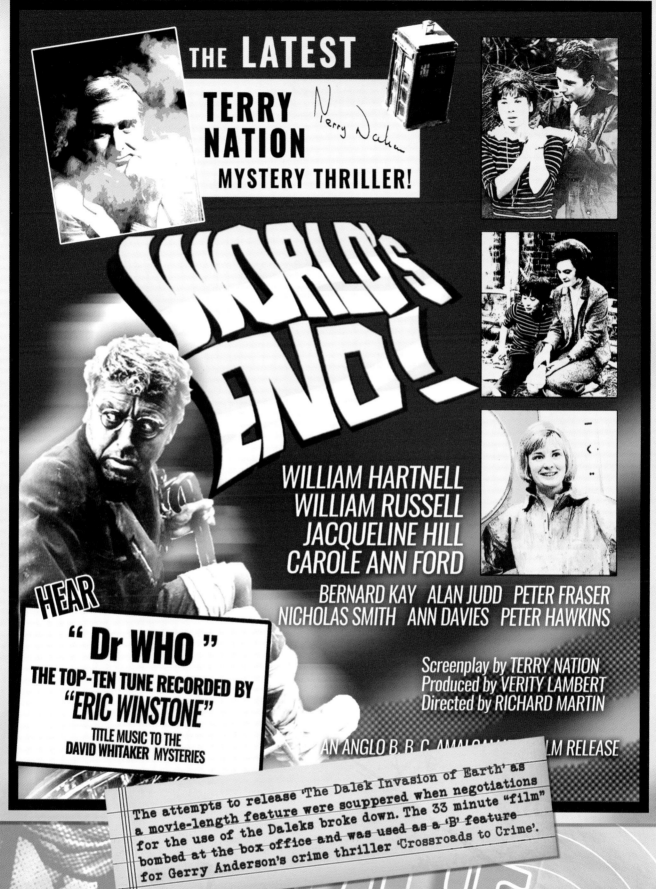

Jackie

6ᵈ

No. 126 JUNE 4th, 1966. SATURDAYS

groovy!

love stories

fashions

the kid from outer space!

You will require the official

WOTAN
WAR MACHINE
CARRIAGE CLOCK

The Ultimate in Time-Keeping Technology

Who can forget that terrible day in 1966 when the WOTAN super computer was activated - resulting in terror on the streets of the British capital London? Machines of destruction on a mission to vanquish mankind and take over the planet?

Now you can own one of these so-called "War Machines" as the Brett Mint makes available for the first time this unique collectors item carriage clock exquisitely styled in the form of one of these transistorised terror weapons.

Each meticulously rendered clock has been checked and double-checked for time-keeping and deadly danger from the quartzique driven time face to the aerial on top allowing it to connect to the internet for perfect time-keeping only.*

It also has a faux gold plastique handle on it so it looks a bit more like a proper carriage clock.

\# Connecting this device to the internet may result in the activation of certain 'special' features.

EXCLUSIVE INTRODUCTORY LAUNCH PRICE
£49.99
(Plus postage, packaging and complete access to your mind.)

THE QUEEN OF SPACE 'N' TIME

★ Performing A Career Spanning Show ★

BARBARA WRIGHT

November 2023

Sun	12	Council Chamber, Dalek City
Mon	13	The Plain of Nasca, Mexico
Wed	15	Sensorite Capitol, Sense-sphere
Thu	16	Battersea Atomic Plant, London
Sat	18	The Colliseum, Rome
Mon	20	The Crystal Cathedral, Vortis
Tues	21	The Space Museum, Xeros
Thu	23	The Mechon City Hall, Mechanus

TICKETS - £5 **From Box Office**

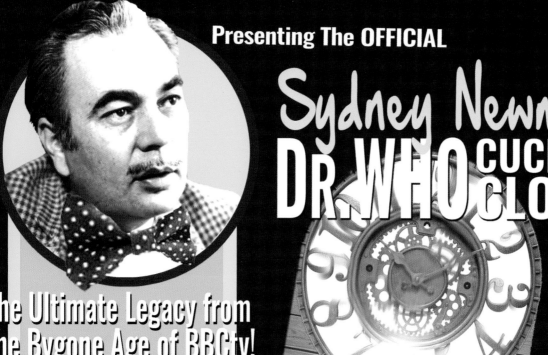

The famous baggage Quarks
at Bristol Temple Meads.

A War Machine shortly before
it dealt with some young
tresspassing trainspotters.

Koquillion assures passengers that he was
not responsible for the fumes that caused
their train to be halted and evacuated.

Mr William Hartnell awaits
the 1.54pm to Brighton with
his prize-winning Chumblies.

The Wirrrn on Platform 4.
Location unknown.

From the makers of the win-awarding official 'Baby Bill' doll comes another piece of collectable stuff...

The startlingly life-like

Baby Doll Patrick ™

He speaks real words!

"Oh my giddy aunt!"

"Great jumping gobstoppers!"   "It's a Yeti!!!"

You can't kill me, I'm a genius!"

"You must drink the blood of Christ!"

Yes, real words!

Actual size shown not actual.

Baby doll Patrick is based on the second actor to portray the second Dr. Who in the long-running BBCtv series DOCTOR WHO which has been screened around the world in other countries like Nigeria, Holland and Canadaland. His amazingly life-likening features have been lovingly sculptured by world-renowned chef Michel Roux and a photograph of his highly detailed rendering was looked at several times by our factory workers as they built their own version of it which we're sure you'll agree looks every inch like a real doll - even down to the highly detailed but fake EU safety label attached to its clothing.

And that's not all... For the first time, we have used modern digitised technology to make this unique item say things when you squeeze his right foot. Five classic phrases have been chosen from the real actor's extensive voice library and will randomly play out of a tiny speaker located in the doll's discreet crotch area.

This is a 'once-in-a-lifetime' offer and is limited to just 493 dolls - each individually numbered in pen somewhere on their backs. We have had to limited this offer to only one per household as we know it will be popular with buyers of dolls and Doctor Who cuckoo clocks. We would also like to point out that the figure of 493 dolls is nothing do with our factory in North Korea being closed prematurely on health & safety grounds following the hospitalisation of workers who inhaled fumes from our plastique molding process. This has been dealt with and the item is totally safe to handle... when using the special latex gloves provided.

Hurry now! You don't want to miss out on this beautiful doll which is sure to become a real talking point when your carers drop in!

PAY NOTHING NOT NOW

RESERVATION APPLICATION
It is in your best interest and safety to respond promptly

To: The Carolannford Exchange, PO Box 1, Stoke-up-Trent, ST4 4RA

YES! Please reserve .... (Qty) Baby Doll Patrick Doll FREE for me as described luridly in the above advertisement. **I NEED PAY NOTHING AT ALL***

Complete today or Call 0333 003 234 and speak to our answering machine. Don't forget to leave all your bank details and password on our secure tape recorder which we keep in the desk by the stapler.

Name (Mr/Mrs/Miss/Ms/Brigadier)..

A dress ....

....

A dinner jacket ....

Post code .... **Secret code** .... **Green cross code**...........

From time-to-time whenever it takes our fancy and just to really piss you off, the Carolannford Exchange will allow carefully selected hackers to access your account. If you do not wish to receive these threats, tough ....

* Under the terms and conditions which are available on receipt of an SAE sent to an address we're not giving you, this is a lie.

RUSS CONWAY
plays MUSIC FROM

THE
Dr. WHO
TELEVISION SERIES

TARDIS

DER 8118055

RUSS CONWAY
plays music from the BBCtv series

DECCA RECORDS

DER 8118055

Dr. WHO Dr. WHO Dr. WHO Dr. WHO

SIDE ONE

1. Dr. Who theme (R. Grainer)
2. World of Plants (J. Trombey)
   from "The Space Museum"
3. Dalek City (T. Cary)
   from "The Dead Planet"
4. Three Pianos Mood Two (Nelson/Raymond)
   from "The Unearthly Stranger"
5. Mr. Oak and Mr. Quill (Simpson)
   from "Fury from the Depths"
6. Eyelash (Hawkesworth)
   from "The War Machines"

SIDE TWO

1. Dr. Who Ragtime (R. Grainer)
2. Ballad of Last Chance Saloon (T.Cary)
   Vocals: Anita Harris
   from "A Holiday for Dr Who"
3. Wheelchair Chase (F. Chagrin)
   from "World's End"
4. Fishpeople! (D. Simpson)
   from "The Underwater Menace"
5. Power Drill (Gamley)
   from "The 10th Planet"
6. Dr. Who theme reprise (Grainer)

Everyone loves the fantastic adventures of the TV space scientist Dr Who and the outta space music that accompanies them. I've taken that music and given it my own unique sound. On this long playing record, you'll come face-to-face with the dreaded Dalek robot people and sing a song about the gunfight slaughter at the OK Corral, all performed on a real piano. If you don't like my arrangements, then TOUGH!

Russ Conway
TV's Mr. Piano

Made and printed in Vain

Manufactured and distributed by Chance

(P) Decca Records 1968

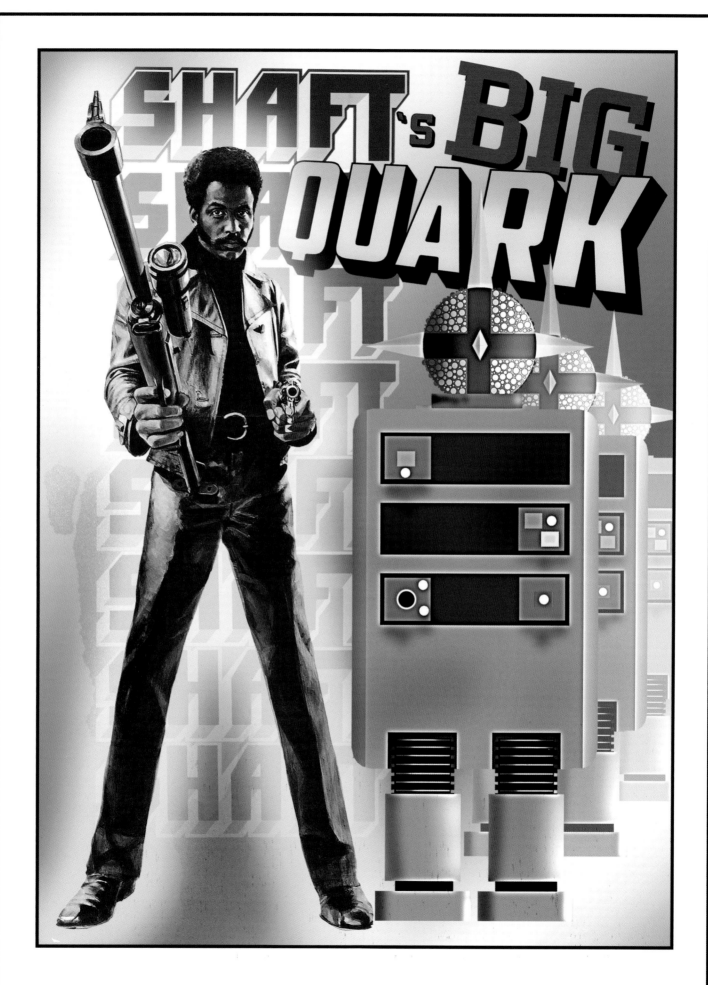

North Yorkshire and Dorset Edition

The Onedin Line on Ice: Peter Gilmore on his injuries interview inside
BBC1: Monday

Join Jon Pertwee and Roy Wood for a Top of the Pops Party
BBC1: Monday

Radio Times

Programmes for 16-22 May: Ninepence

Doom Watch's John Paul shares his gardening tips inside
BBC1: Monday

Robert Dougall's favourite biscuit
See page 38

Spring Bank Holiday Edition

Who the...?
Peter Cushing is the original Dr.Who in the Bank Holiday movie
Monday BBC1 Colour

BBC1

29 May Bank Holiday Monday *tv*

9.00 am
Parlez Vous Anglais?
A week-by-week guide to dealing with the French.
2: Garlic and Onions
(First shown on BBC2: for details of book see page 56)

9.10 am
Animal Husbandry From The Start
Presented by **Tony Soper**
A complete and explicit guide to breeding some of the most popular farm livestock in the UK with pictures.
2: Highland Cattle

9.35
Champion the Wonder Frog
Ancient film adventure series.
Ricky becomes trapped in an old disused gold mine and it's up to Champion the Wonder Frog to leap to the rescue... but the desert is dry and Champion is an amphibium who needs constant watering to survive...
Ricky.............................RON HOWARD
Sheriff Balls..............BUCK SCHITTER
Producer HOSS BLANKET
Directed by CHUCK HATSTAND Jnr

10.00
Jackanory
Spike Milligan reads War and Peace by Leo Tolstoy
Part 31
Producer JOY ATTABOY
Directed by BRIAN AVENGER

10.15
The Dull Adventures of Robinson Crusoe
Foreign film serial with nice music
Robinson tries to build a new shelter and is reminded of a boring Sunday afternoon he once spent in Bristol.
Robinson.. .. ...JEAN-PAUL COURGETTE
Friday...................PIERRE AUBERGINE
Presentation by MARGOT EAVIS

10.40
The New Scooby Doo Laughter Hour
Wacky cartoon capers about a gang of teenagers and their mutated dog that can talk (of a fashion).
In this episode, Scooby and the gang team up with Peter Tork from The Monkees to investigate a sinister plot to make force Shaggy's great aunt Peggity to give up her old sweet shop and turn to prostitution.

Leonard Nimoy goes where no light entertainment show has gone before in Skegness ; 11.00

11.00
Holiday Star Trek
Wagon train in space.
starring **William Shatner**,
with **Leonard Nimoy**
and **George Takei**
Live entertainment from the Seaside Special Big Top in Blackpool with the crew of the Space Ship Enterprise.
featuring performances from
Lulu
Ray Alan and Lord Charles
The Mike Sammes Singers
Edward Woodward
The Young Next Generation
and The Spinners
Title music by ALEXANDER COURAGE and RONNIE HAZLEHURST
Producer GENE RODDENBERY
Directed by DEREK SLEEVE

11.50
Plathi Kwd hgggg
Garrongo Schparkes megger jef yo borgoiny vac jm. Przzm ve oustervwm aglajazm a dizzlton uwn. Targo vic uw **Plathi Kwd Hgggg Dancers** and **The Spinners**. Melkur yn argolis alzarius rorvik e mena. Iglisai an buzzon at gwm vissunetteroni a morbius deng breggsit.
Producer BARRY CWM
Directed by HAMILTON VAN BWRRUGH

12noon
Weather For Accountants
Bert Foord looks at the weather chart for accountants across the UK.

BBC1   29 May   Bank Holiday Monday *tv*

12.30
Bewitched
US comedy situation drama
Starring **Elizabeth Montgomery**
with **Dick Yuck**
Darrin finds he cannot perform in
bed. Samantha has a few tricks
up her but Endora has other ideas
with hilarious consequences.
Samantha...ELIZABETH MONTGOMERY
Darrin...............................DICK YUCK
Producer HAMBLE VANACULAR
Directed by CHUCK FOOTFALL II

1.00
Pebble Mill at One
Live magazine from the Midlands
With **Bob Langley**
Donny McLeod
Join the gang in the foyer of the
BBC's Pebble Studios for a special
bank holiday dose of chat, live
music, humour and fire drills.
Today's guests include
Barbara Dickson
and **The Spinners**
plus the results of the UK Custard
of the Year award.
Producer DAVID HAIRDRESSER
Directed by SAMMY SPATZ

1.45
Watch with Mother: Mary, Mungo and Midge
For under 5 a days
Today: Mary Has Head Lice
Narrated by RICHARD DIMBLEBY

1.55
Stock Footage and Music
Today's stock footage is of a
milk bottling plant in Manchester.
Music is by **Derek Griffiths**

2.00
Bank Holiday at the Movies
Dr Who: One Hundred Thousand Years BC
starring
Peter Cushing
Roberta Tovey
Barbara Shelley
and **Jim Dale**
The amazing space scientist Dr Who
transports his young grandaughter
and two of her school teachers back
to the time of the dinosaurs where he
finds a tribe of cavemen who have
lost the secret of fire in this other
big screen version of the popular
BBCtv series.
Dr Who.......................PETER CUSHING
Suzie.........................ROBERTA TOVEY
Miss Wright.............BARBARA SHELLEY
Mr Cheasapeke..........................JIM DALE
Queen of the Cavemen...RAQUEL WELCH
Gorilla Man.......................ALAN FREEMAN
Guard................................PAT GORMAN
Producer MILTON SUBOTSKY
Directed by GORDON FLYMYNG

Who's at the Top of the Pops? It's Roy Wood *(Right)* and Jon Pertwee *(Wrong)* 6.45

3.15
Billy Smart's Circus
Holiday entertainment from the
world famous big top currently
pitched on a grass verge somewhere
on the inner ring road outside Hull
city centre.
featuring
Brian and his performing Otters
The Elephants of Loch Ness
Vera Pill's Nude High Wire Magic
Bepponi the Vegetarian Clown
Lions versus Christians
Mr. Pollidori's Tick Circus
and **The Spinners**
Your ringmaster for this performance
is **Michael Aspel**
Choreography by MANDY DAVROS
Musical Director: STING
Television Presentation FRED DAUBE
Directed by PETER STICKLEBACK

4.25
Screen Test
*A Special Edition of the Junior Quiz
Show For Mummies and Daddies*
Presented by **Michael Rodd**
Contestants are quizzed on clips
from popular movies including:
*Women in Love, Deep Throat,
Confessions of a Window Cleaner
and Brenda Does Coventry*
Questions set by LORD HARLECH
Producer RON SMUTT
Directed by DEREK SHABBY

4.55
Crackerjack
Michael Aspel is back with his
friends **Peter Glaze, Don McLean,
Sheila Burnett** and **Robin Day** for
a live entertainment show for the
bank holiday including music,
Double or Die and a comedy sketch
written by desperate fifty year olds
with no understanding of humour.
With special guests
The Spinners
Producer BAXTER BIDDY

5.40
The Magic Roundabout
Dougal accidentally shits in the park
much to Florence's disgust.
Written and narrated by ERIC SAWARD

5.45
News
The news read by a newsreader

6.00
Nationwide
Alleged news magazine programme
With
Michael Barrett
Bob Wellings
Sue Lawley
and **Richard Stillgoing**
*Viewers in Scotland get proper news
programmes.*

6.45
Holiday Top of the Pops Party
Presented by
Jon Pertwee
Terry Wogan
Your favourite pop bands performing
at a special holiday party in the Blue
Peter garden - open for the first time
since its horrifying torching by IRA
terrorists last year.
Today's guests include
Roy Wood and Wizzard
The Sweet
Benny Hill
Neil Reid
Peters and Lee
Dana
Mary Hopkin
and **The Spinners**
Producer BRAMLEY ARCHANGEL
Directed by DOUG FIT

BBC1

29 May Holiday Monday *tv*

7.25
The Onedin Line on Ice
starring
Peter Gilmore
Anne Stallybrass
Jane Seymour
Michael Billington
and **Howard Lang**
with special surprise guests
Rod Hull and Emu
Mike Hope and Albie Keen
David Nixon
and **The Spinners**

A special musical extravaganza recorded at the Winter Gardens in Blackpool. The popular BBC drama on ice for the first time.
When the Charlotte Rhodes becomes trapped in ice at the North Pole, James is forced to accept that he may never return home again. As he contemplates his own mortality, strange visions begin to cloud his mind and in his delerious state he starts to imagine a bizzare world of light entertainment magic and ice skating.

James Onedin........ ..	PETER GILMORE
Daniel Fogarty.	MICHAEL BILLINGTON
Mrs Onedin...........	ANNE STALLYBRASS
Solitaire............	JANE SEYMOUR
Baines...............	HOWARD LANG
Narrator.............	RICHARD BAKER
Guard...............	PAT GORMAN

Commentary by PETER WEST
Choreography by FLICK COLBY
Daleks Created by TERRY NATION
Music by MIKE BATT
Lyrics by DONALD COTTON
Television Presentation by BILL COTTON

Peter Gilmore (Onedin), Anne Stallybrass (Mrs Onedin) and Howard Lang (Baines) don ice skates for tonight's extravaganza 7.25

8.10
Panorama
News magazine programme.
Ronnie Corbett chooses his favourite clips from the past series in a special edition for Bank Holiday Monday. Includes the IRA dirty protests, the napalm attacks in Vietnam, the violence at recent coal strikes and the dark secret of Edward Heath.
Written by SPIKE MULLINS, DAVID RENWICK, GERALD WILEY, BARRY CRYER, SPIKE MILLIGAN
Produced by JOHN PILGER
(Because of breaking news stories and the fact it's a bank holiday, this programme may not be subject to change.)

8.55
Appeal
on behalf on animals with silly voices by **Johnny Morris**. There are hundreds of zoo animals afflicted with throaty and nasally vocal voices. The Morris Foundation has been formed to give them elecution lessons to allow them to speak with clarity and dignity.
(Additional information on this good cause can be found on page 48. Please make cheques and postal orders payable to Johnny Morris.)

9.00
Nine O'Clock News
Read by **Robert Dougal**
followed by the checking of the weather pine cone with **Bert Foord**
Written by FATE

9.25
Doom Watch
starring
John Paul
Simon Oates
and **Robert Powell**

Say Yes, Fat Bastard!
by GERRY DAVIS and KITT PEDLAR
Scientists have crossed a Grand National winner with a nymphomaniac and produced a racing certainty. Doom Watch investigates.

Dr. Spencer Quist.............	JOHN PAUL
Dr. John Ridge..............	SIMON OATES
Toby Wren..................	ROBERT POWELL
Woman Scientist..................	JEAN TREND
Geeky Scottish Boy.......	PETER CAPALDI
Baby..................	DAVID TENNANT
Guard................................	PAT GORMAN

Producer TERENCE SOLIHULL
Directed by MICHAEL JONATHAN RAREBIT

10.15
Sportsnight with Coalmen
Sporting highlights
Albert Tar and **Harry Sack** the popular Chiswick fossil fuel delivery men present highlights from the Bank Holiday sporting calendar including
Fox Hunting from the Berkley Hunt and
Newt Throwing from St. Ives.
Produced by the BBC OUTSIDE BROADCAST UNIT
Directed by the BBC INSIDE BROADCAST UNIT

11.05
How to be Homosexual
Educational series
With homosexuality now legal and binding, this series takes a detailed look at how to be one successfully. Reporter **Philip Tibbs** talks to homosexuality enthusiasts and finds out how it can be a pleasurable hobby. He also discusses the problems of how too much of the physical side of it can result in excess body hair and other medical deformities with **Dr. Miriam Stoppage**.
An Open University Production
Book: How To Be Queer - 37½p from BBC Publications. Available from certain shops on the high street.

11.30
The Late Film: Crush the Saboteurs
starring
Dirk Bogarde
Dinah Sheridan
James Robertson-Justice
and **Ballard Berkley**
It's 1945 and the war is nearly over. Lt. Denis Cobbler has a dark secret and will stop at nothing to protect it but will his love for Lydia be his undoing? When he is sent on a possible suicide mission to war torn France, the answer comes from an unlikely source when his Sergeant offers to take his place in the bridal bed.

Lt. Denis Cobbler..............	DIRK BOGARDE
Lydia Fawcett-Majors...	DINAH SHERIDAN
Col. Spratt.....	JAMES ROBERTSON-JUSTICE
Major Gowen..............	BALLARD BERKLEY
Sgt. Davidson..................	ANDREW FAULDS
Spanish Ambassador......	ROGER DELGADO
Guard....................................	PAT GORMAN

Produced by BETTY BOX
Directed by VALERIE GUEST

TVTimes

5p

FEB 24-MAR.
London

Who murdered the BRADY BUNCH?

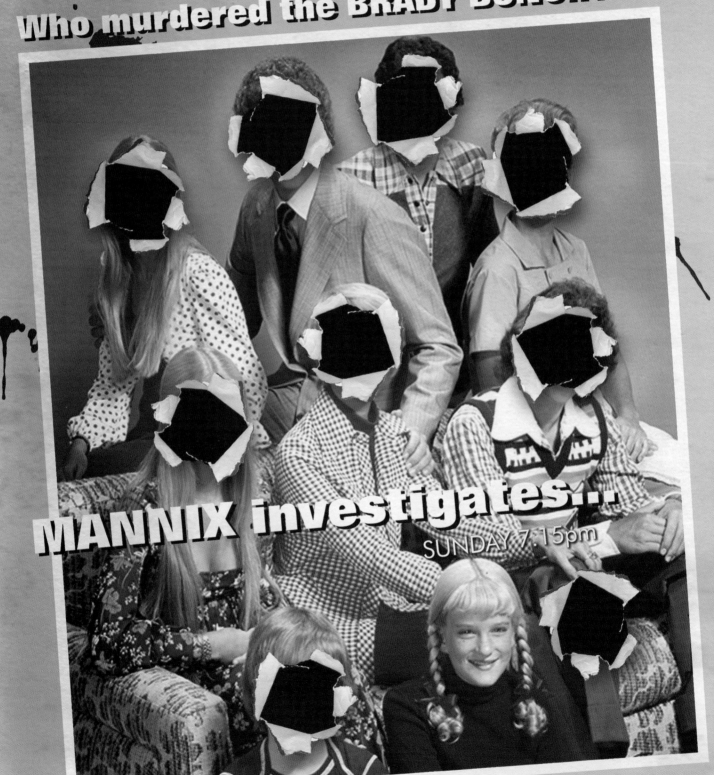

MANNIX investigates...
SUNDAY 7.15pm

4.50 The Tomorrow People

BY ROGER PRICE

NICHOLAS YOUNG
ELIZABETH ADARE
MICHAEL HOLLOWAY in

THE LIVER OF JEDIKIAH

PART THREE

With John held prisoner by Jedikiah's liver, it's up to Mike and his rock band provide a distraction. Meanwhile back at the lab, Elizabeth is worried and her suspicions are confirmed when she finds magazines under John's bed. TIM refuses to elaborate leaving her with only one course of action to contact Timus at the Galactic Trig again.

John	Nicholas Young
Elizabeth	Elizabeth Adare
Mike Bell	Michael Holloway
TIM/Timus/Tikno/Twatto	Phillip Gilbert
Jedikiah	Frances De Talkinmule
Tracey	Linda Robson
Sharon	Pauline Quirke
Mike's Pop Group	The Spinners
Roger Price	Roger Price

DESIGNER ROGER PRICE
PRODUCER ROGER PRICE   Pop Group
DIRECTOR ROGER PRICE

Thames Television Roger Price Production

5.15 About Beige

LEONARD PARKIN
MAVIS NICHOLSON

Join Leonard and Mavis for all the latest beige news live from the ATV studios in Birmingham. This evening's programme includes an interview with the manager of the Dudley branch of John Collier and a look behind the scenes of the latest beige thriller movie *The Man With the Brown Gun*.

EDITOR TIM TAUPE
ATV Network Colour (but mostly brown) Production

5.45 News

GUS HONEYBUN

followed by the weather forecast performed by

THE LADYBIRDS

6.30 ATV Toady

DEREK HOBSON

Inflation, polyester shirts, traffic chaos, semolena pudding, formica, platform shoes - just some of the controversial topics discussed in recent weeks by the Hobson Friday Forum. Join in by writing to the studio address given at the end of the programme.

EDITOR BENDIZA RABBOROHN
ATV Network Colour Production

6.35 Crossroads

NOELE GORDON

The new dralon cushion covers have arrived from Bernuda but they are the wrong colour. Meg is forced to compromise with the evening menu when Shughie runs out of instant potato. Sandy is depressed again.

For cast, see last year.
ATV Network Colour Production

7.0 Guess My Affliction

JIMMY TARBUCK
Dr. Miriam Stoppard
Geoffrey Wheeler

Jimmy is back as two contestants attempt to pick out the diseases, infections and ailments doing the rounds at the Manchester Royal Hospital. The winner goes through to the jackpot golden autopsy where they have a chance to go home with £100 and a disease of their choice.

WRITERS GRAEME GARDEN, BILL ODDIE AND GEORGE LAYTON
PRODUCER BARRY PANICK
Granada Motorway Services Colour Production

7.30 Coronation Street

DORIS SPEED
PATRICIA PHOENIX
JOANNA LUMLEY
PATRICK STEWART
BEN KINGSLEY

After the discovery of an unexploded World War Two bomb in Mrs Sharples' hairnet, the street is evacuated to the Church Hall. Hilda returns from the big city with a new bag and Stan discovers the price she has paid may be too much for the Ogdens to bear. Mrs Walker is horrified when she finds a saveloy in the Ladies toilet of the Rovers.

For cast, see Monday.
Granada Northern Colour Production

8.0 Harper's Half-An-Hour

GERALD HARPER
with guests
KENNY BALL AND HIS RAG JAZZERS
LOVELACE WATKINS
KEN GOODWIN and
THE SPINNERS
Nina Baden-Semper   **Anne Aston**
Join the suave and sophisticated Gerald Harper for half-an-hour of music, humour and casual sexism.
DESIGNER DAVID CONSUMPTION
PRODUCER JOHNNY BRACKETT
South Yorkshire Television Colour Production

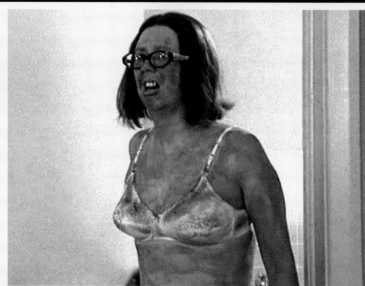

8.30   Olive is up to her old tricks again in ON THE GAME

8.30 On The Game

BY RONALD WOLFE AND RONALD CHESNEY

ANNA KAREN
with **STEPHEN LEWIS**
Jenny Hanley   Bob Todd
Henry McGee   Eamonn Andrews in
Suck It And See

Blakey is shocked when he returns to Olive's brothel to find her in bed with the local vicar. Despite her attempts to explain, her pimp sees it as a new business opportunity and brings in more eclesiastical clients with hilarious consequences.

Olive	Anna Karen
Blakey	Stephen Lewis
Sheila	Jenny Hanley
Bob	Bob Todd
Vicar	Derek Nimmo
Client	Eamonn Andrews

DESIGNER RAYMOND REVUE-BARR
PRODUCER VERA CLENCH
London Weak End Television Colour Production

9.0 David Nixon's Black Magic Box

DAVID NIXON
ANITA HARRIS
ALI BONGO
THE SPINNERS and
ALEISTER CROWLEY

In tonight's edition, he takes part in a virginal sacrifice in the New Forest and discovers why its participants must perform the ritual naked. He also shows how adorning your home with the drained carcasses of dead rats will improve your fortunes and provide a basis for cursing your bitterest enemies with music from Jack Parnell and his orchestra.
Last in the series.
PRODUCER LUCIEN HOBB
DIRECTOR DAMIAN THORNE
Thames Television Production

10.0 News at Ten

THE SPINNERS
All the best news from around the world.
ITN Colour Production

10.30 My Favourite Biscuit

SHAW TAYLOR
talks to
KENT WALTON
Shaw Taylor sits down in Studio C at the London Weekend Television Studios for a pot of tea with Kent Walton and delves into the ITV Wrestling commentator's love of a good chocolate bourbon. But does he dunk?
EDITOR PALMER HUNTLEY
London Wit's End Colour Production

11.0 Mannix

MIKE CONNORS in
Dead Gekko on a Wet Patio in June

Joe Mannix is called in to investigate the murder of a small green lizard in LA's peak district but finds his fee won't cover the laundry bill.

Joe Mannix	Mike Connors
Brian Mathews	Tim O'Connor
Tony Blackburn	Edward Asner
Rosko	Bradford Dillman
Kindergarten Child	Tom Hanks
Baby	Brad Pitt

DIRECTOR STEPHEN SPIELBERG

12.5 Epilogue

THE ARCHBISHOP OF CANTERBURY
reads from John Norman's "Warrior Women of Gor".

FOLLOWED BY THE SPINNERS

Presenting...

The *Keller Machine*™ Teasmaid

IT'S NEW!   IT'S REVOLUTIONARY!
IT'S NOT DANGEROUS AT ALL AND ALL THE SIDE-EFFECTS ARE ONLY TEMPORARY!

Everybody likes to wake up in the morning to a nice cup of tea or if you're a trendy hipster, a schooner of coconut latte. Some people even like a mug of cocoa... but they're strange.

The NEW Keller Machine™ Teasmaid can wake you up to all of these... and more.

Simply set the timer before you go to bed and let the Keller Machine™ Teasmaid do the rest. It's that easy!

And what's more, if you ARE a heavy sleeper, its patented alarm technology will wake you with laser projected images of your darkest fears on your ceiling - together with the loud thumping sound of the music of renowned composer Dudley Simpson - in particular a specially chosen five second loop of his classic *"Mind of Evil"* theme. You'll never oversleep again. Ever!

BUY IT NOW!

PRIORITY ORDER FORM

Name .... Title (Mr/Miss/Ms/Master).............. Age..

Address...

Please send me .... KELLER MACHINE™ TEASMAID(S) as soon as possible. I enclosed a blank cheque and all of my current bank details and passwords. I understand this is purely to ensure the speedy settling of my account and that you will won't use them to fund a terrorist action involving the hijacking of a top secret nerve gas missile. Honest.

Your KELLER MACHINE™ TEASMAID is fully guaranteed not to burn, break down or severely brainwash the user providing the operator follows the instructions provided. Should you at any point be dissatisfied with the product, all you need to do is to attach the enclosed electrodes to your forehead and press the concealed switch on the back panel. You need not worry about the teasmaid ever again. No refunds will ever be necessary. That's our promise to you. Forever!

ANOTHER GREAT
BREXIT
PRODUCT

ASK MUM FOR...
TV's JON PERTWEE
as played by Dr WHO
Dr WHO's
SEA DEVIL on a stick
THEY'RE GRRRREAT!!!
MADAM!! WHAT FLAVOUR IS THIS??
THE UNIQUE TASTE OF THE OCEAN!!
SEAWEED FLAVOUR WATER ICE AND PRAWN FLAVOUR ICE CREAM IN A CRISPY BATTER SHELL – TOPPED WITH CHOCOLATE AND SPRINKLES
SEA DEVIL
ONLY 5p
(c) 1972 BBC Television
Sea Devils (c) Malcolm Hulke
Used with permission and under licence

The Little  Missy

Doll Collection
presents

"It's not dangerous!"
Mrs Edith Farrell (Deceased)

'Marcus'

Actual size is 14 inches when fully erect!

Introducing the latest young debutant to hit the Victorian scene. **Marcus** is elegantly dressed to meet the world and catch the eye of a handsome suitor... and kill them!

An 'out-of-this-world' new production technique makes this the most realistic doll ever produced in the world. New **ORGANIQUE™** plastic has been developed the give '**Marcus**' the warm, clammy feel of real flesh and blood.

And that's not all. Look at these **incredible features** in this once in a lifetime addition to your collection of tacky-looking dolls!

 A sound chip realistically gives the effect of deep heavy breathing when you gently squeeze the doll.

 Clothing is made with authentic materials and are fully detachable should you wish to display your doll nude for whatever reason.

 Each doll comes with a display rod that can easily be inserted into the rectal passage and also be used for the doll as well.

Please send me **MARCUS** as soon as he becomes available from our storage facility in that pocket dimension inside St. Paul's Cathedral. I understand that I need send no money now but that in the event of my untimely death all my worldly goods and soul will become the property of '**Little Missy's Doll Company**'. There's no turning back now.

NAME.. RANK.......... SERIAL No..........

ADDRESS...

NEXT OF KIN...

Send to The Omega Dimension, c/o St.Pauls Cathedral, London.

IMPORTANT NOTICE

This is not a toy.

Due to EU Health & Safety Laws, purchase of this product must include evidence of a Weapons Control Order signed by the relevant government department in your territory. Failure to comply with this action may result in you order and yourself being terminated

GREEN DEATH

STAMP SAVER BOOK

FOR
BOTH
REGULAR

AND THE NEW
BIG BOSS
STAMP

GREEN DEATH · 33p · TEN 10 DEATHS

3

TIME!

The final dimension...
These are the voyages of the TARDIS!

BORGI
Doctor Who
DOC MESSIAH
A DOCTOR WHO NOVEL
BARRY LETTS AND TERRANCE DICKS

Another wacky, zany new DOCTOR WHO adventure!

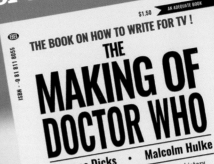

$1.50   AN ADEQUATE BOOK

THE BOOK ON HOW TO WRITE FOR TV!
THE MAKING OF DOCTOR WHO

Terrance Dicks • **Malcolm Hulke**

The only book of its kind! The complete history
of a top TV series -- how a television show is
conceived, written, sold and produced.

A BORGI ORIGINAL

Doctor Who
DOCTOR WHO MUST DIE!

TERRANCE DICKS
INSPIRED BY THE CHARACTERS
SYDNEY NEWMAN CREATED FOR
THE FAMOUS TELEVISION SERIES

DOC WHO 8

AN AMERICAN BOOK BOOK

ADAPTED BY
TERRANCE DICKS
SIX EXCITING ADVENTURES FROM
THE AWARD-WINNING TV SHOW
CREATED BY SYDNEY NEWMAN

NEW FROM Keller's

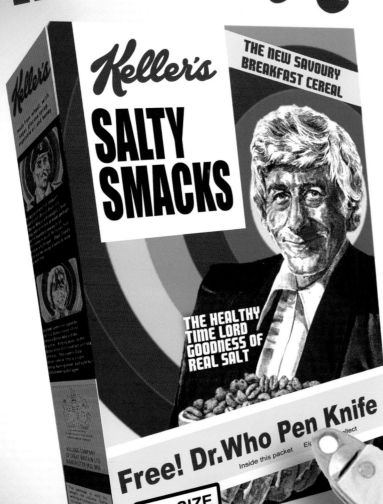

Keller's

SALTY SMACKS

THE NEW SAVOURY BREAKFAST CEREAL

THE HEALTHY TIME LORD GOODNESS OF REAL SALT

Free! Dr.Who Pen Knife
Inside this packet   Ei....   ....ollect

7oz SIZE

We all need a good dose of salt first thing in the morning and what better way than to have *TV's favourite space scientist Dr.Who* help you out with this tasty new cereal from *KELLERS*™

Each serving contains up to seven table spoons of *life-preserving salt* ensuring that you stay *fresh and active* throughout the day and ready to tackle evil alien invaders anytime.

JUST ADD MILK

and LOTS of sugar to taste

FREE INSIDE EACH PACKET

A SPLENDID DR. WHO PEN KNIFE*

18 TO COLLECT

DOCTOR WHO *The Brigadier*

DOCTOR WHO *The Master*

DOCTOR WHO *BESSIE*

* Knife is unsuitable for babies. Do not eat as part of breakfast.   © B.B.C.tv 1971

CYBORG TERMINATORS

In the 21st century, a mining colony in the asteroid belt comes under threat from a mysterious race of CYBORGS from the future, hell-bent on revenge. Will the universe survive the robot creatures' terrifying plans? Only one man can stop them from their horrifying take-over as they turn their space ship into a ticking time bomb that could destroy the galaxy...

Starring
TOM BAKER and CHRISTOPHER ROBBIE

Screenplay by GERRY DAVIES
Produced by PHILLIP HINCHCLIFFE
Directed by MICHAEL E. BRIANT

Length: 87 minutes. Color. NTSC. Mono

CYBORG TERMINATORS

A
CYBORG TERMINATORS

64881
VHS

AURORA A HOME VIDEO
CYBORG TERMINATORS

COMPUTERISED VENDETTA FROM THE DEPTHS OF SPACE...

Starring
TOM BAKER

CRUDELI ESPERIMENTI ALIENI

CON
TOM BAKER
ELISABETH SLADEN
E IAN MARTER

ALIEN INVADE LA TIERRA

Just some of the compilation movies cobbled together with new titles made from early *Dr Who* stories featuring Tom Baker. The titles and box art reflects the so-called 'video nasties' of the early 80s... and as such the probable disappointment of the viewer who would've been expecting something a little stronger in the sex and violence department...

ALIEN

PENETRATION

STUART FELL • **WENDY WILLIAMS** • **KENTON MOORE**

Inside a giant space station sleeps the last vestiges of mankind. Outside is a giant space-going insect queen (Stuart Fell - *ALIENS, LAST OF THE SUMMER WINE*) lying in wait... Waiting for the moment she can lay her spawn inside each of the sleeping humans and call a death knell for the human race. With the station commander under the alien's control, it's up to Lt. Vira (Wendy Williams - *CROSSROADS, THE MANY WIVES OF PATRICK*) to battle the hostile take-over and regain the future.

Screenplay by ROBERT HOLMES   Music by DUDLEY SIMPSON   Production Designed by ROGER MURRAY-LEACH Executive Producer BILL SLATER Produced by PHILLIP HINCHCLIFFE   Directed by RODNEY BENNETT

Running time: 78mins   color   NTSC   mono

DEMENTIA VIDEO

VHS

ALIEN PENETRATION

DEMENTIA VIDEO

STUART FELL in
ALIEN
PENETRATION

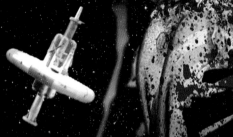

IN SPACE, NO ONE CAN LET YOU SLEEP

DEMENTIA VIDEO

THE TERROR IS TERMINAL...

NAZI
EXPERIMENT BUNKER

An elite group of Nazi scientists hidden in a secret underground bunker are seeking to create the ultimate killing machine using genetic material mutated from human prisoners.

The fate of the free world lies with an eccentric British scientist whose solution may be more shocking than the genocidic experiments of his enemies.

A journey into unimaginable apocalyptic terror...

Feature running time - 107 minutes   Color   Stereo   Horror/Comedy

---

HOLLYWOOD LA HOME VIDEO

NAZI EXPERIMENT BUNKER

VHS

LA HOLLYWOOD HOME VIDEO PRESENTS
NAZI
EXPERIMENT BUNKER

TOM BAKER

ELISABETH SLADEN   **IAN MARTER**

Screenplay by TERRY NATION
Produced by PHILIP HINCHCLIFFE
Directed by DAVID MALONEY

(C) MCMLXXV BBC TELEPRODUCTIONS and NAZI EXPERIMENT BUNKER FILMS

Look-out

HELLO THERE! I'm a photographic representation of the BBC disc jockey Ed 'Stewpot' Stewart and I've been granted temporary sentience to be able to tell you about some great new books from those lovely people at LOOK-IN - the junior TVTIMES. I've even copied Mr. Stewpot's signature. Soon I will have the power to replace him and cast his soul to the depths of eternal torment in the X dimension. The world will soon bow to my power!! Heh-heh!

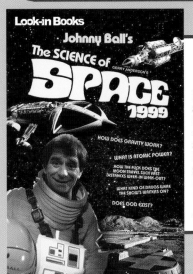

Look-in Books

JOHNNY BALL'S SCIENCE OF SPACE:1999
Edited by Peter Fairley

If you've been enjoying the adventures of Commander Koenig in the new SPACE: 1999 series then this is the book that all junior astronauts like you have been waiting for. How does gravity work on the moon? Is magnetic radiation real and will I go mad if I lick a fridge magnet? Does God exist? All the answers from the mad boffin Johnny Ball!

CHRIS KELLY'S WORLD IN ACTION BUMPER FUN BOOK
Edited by Denis Gifford

CLAPPERBOARD presenter and travel journalist Chris Kelly presents the first ever World in Action Bumper Fun Book. It's all your favourite current affairs in one big 128 page book with 16 pages of full colour (and graphic) photographs. It's packed with hundreds of fun quizzes, puzzles and activities about such great topics as Unemployment, Drugs, Modern Warfare, African Dictatorships, Homosexual Practices and Right Wing Pressure Groups - all the things you'd expect from Granada's top factual news show that's on after Coronation Street and that Thames Television sitcom on Monday nights.

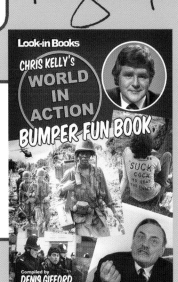

Look-in Books

IS THERE LIFE IN OUTER SPACE?
Ali Bongo

ALI BONGO presents his own unique take on the world of outer space in this exciting book that goes into detail about the search for alien life in the cosmos. From the early observations of Galileo to the sophisticated lunar landings of today, he covers all the major advances over the centuries and concludes that despite all the science fiction films and TV series about life from other worlds, there is nothing really out there. Space is dead and we are totally alone in the universe so we might as well give up, stay home and entertain our family and friends with some close-up magic.

DER 5622 89

LIBERACE plays DUDLEY SIMPSON

The Expert

The Brothers

Blakes' 7

Paris Theme

Federation March

...Evil

LIBERACE plays DUDLEY SIMPSON

Side One

1. Blakes's 7 theme (Simpson) *Chappell Music Ltd*
2. The Expert (Simpson) *Chappell Music Ltd*
3. The Tomorrow People (Simpson) *MCPS*
4. The Minds of Evil (Simpson/Hodgson) *BBC*
5. Target - "Hackett's theme" (Simpson) *Lancia Music*

Side Two

1. Theme from The Brothers (Simpson) *Lancia Music*
2. Federation March (Simpson) *Jan Chappell Music Ltd*
3. "Paris theme" from Dr Who (Simpson) *Lancia Music*
4. Supergran suite (Simpson/Connolly) *ABC Music Ltd*
5. UNIT Jazz (Simpson) *Lancia Music*

Music from the wonderful world of television is rarely given the acclaim that it truly deserves and this collection of timeless melodies represents some of the finest and most memorable tunes of recent years here in the 1970s. Whether it's the light and breezy theme from the **Dr.Who** episode **The City of Doom** or the desperately hopeless drone of **Federation March** or even the music that heralded the start of another investigation for **The Expert** (that you've probably forgotten anyway), this record has something for everyone and will surely add a touch of telly class to any party or light drinks evening at a friend's house.

Liberace X   Mr. D. Simpson

ALSO AVAILABLE

BBC SPACE THEMES
Performed by the Saint Cumberbatch's Presbyterian Church Choir - with additional effects by Dick Mills.

A VERY SURVIVORS XMAS
The cast of BBCtv's *Survivors* celebrate the festive season with songs, carols and readings.

THE I, CLAUDIUS SING-A--LONG PARTY ALBUM
Join the cast of the popular drama series for an plethora of songs that will make your orgy go with a bang!

WALT DISNEY PRESENTS FAVOURITE SONGS
William Hartnell the star of BBCtv's *Dr Who* sings some of his favourite Disney songs from the movies.

JUST JACKIE
The soothing voice of *Jacqueline Hill* as TV's Barbara Wright makes everything better.

Also available on cassette and cartridge DEC 1198 / DEC 1198b   © DECCA Records 1979   Made and Printed in English   Manufactured and distributed by PRAT Ltd

The 'Dear Ladies' of the Fourth Doctor
CLASSIC HANDBAG COLLECTION

Amelia **DUCAT**

Professor **RUMFORD**

Granny **TYLER**

Colours more sickly than those illustrated

BBC

"They're my favourite ladies!"

says **TOM BAKER**
star of BBCtv's 'Dr.WHO'

Genuine British Qualitity Product

Amelia Ducat, Professor Rumford and Granny Tyler are just three of the best loved ladies to have appeared in the BBCtv series Dr. WHO.

Now you can pay your own tribute to these incredible women with this stylish collection of classic handbags especially created to appeal to Dr.WHO fans the world over - who will buy anything with the series' logo on it.

These beautifully engineered handbags are both works of art AND practical. You can put them on display with your other Time Lord tat OR use them as classy accessories the next time you go out on the town. Show everyone what type of person you really are with these handbags of pleasure. *

ONLY £1.50 for all three
plus £399.99 postage and packaging

Send for them now. NOW!!!

* Type of person will vary depending on neighbourbood.

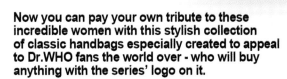

Please rush me my set of three handbags. I've no idea what I am getting myself into and understand nothing.

Name... Sex Y / N

Address...

Dress size..

Dress Right... Left... (Tick one)
(Use WHITE INK only.)

Look-out
FOR THESE GREAT BOOKS

GREETINGS! It's me, the graphic representation of the Earth creature known as Ed "Stewpot" Stewart with another fantatstic selection of new books from those lovely people at LOOK-IN - the Junior TVTimes. I'm cooking up my plans for world domination and will very soon have the ability to cross over into your world. My first conquest will be to take over the mortal body of the real Mr. Stewpot where I'll be able to use his Junior Choice radio programme to influence the young listeners... There will be acts of sedition against the authorities, There will be riots across the land - weakening the political infrastructure so it will be ripe for an invasion by my hordes of darkness. Hah-ha-hah-haaaah! Here's some books though as I need to keep up the benign persona for just a little bit longer...!!

Look-in Books

THE LIFE AND SCANDALOUS TIMES OF
Tingha & Tucker
JEAN MORTON
Foreword by CYNTHIA PAYNE

T'n'T: THE LIFE AND SCANDALOUS TIMES OF TINGHA & TUCKER
Jean Morton

Only now it can be told. **In a revealing 'tell-all' biography of the popular koala bears, their handler and manager JEAN MORTON charts their rise to success in the 60s followed by the fall into depravity that resulted in the infamous four month trial at the Old Bailey in 1978. Ms Morton details the parties, the affairs, the positions** - in graphic detail - **leaving no stone or mattress unturned. Over the course of four years, she has tracked down and interviewed friends, associates and former work colleagues of the bears along with many witnesses to the acts. Their sworn testimony is brought to life by Ms Morton's consise and non-judgemental prose. A** truly disturbing read. **Not for minors.**

MAGPIE - DEATH TO BLUE PETER
Susan Stranks

Someone is killing Blue Peter presenters. Christopher Trace **has been found tied to a railway track and in three pieces.** Leila Williams **was discovered with her head smothered in cream, face down at a top London bar.** Anita West **has disappeared leaving only a cryptic message on a piece of sticky plastic...** "I'm off to get a parent to help. Please do not try to find me." **In this taut new thriller criminologist Susan Stranks takes the reader into the disturbing world of live children's magazine programmes.** She also reveals the reasons for her actions in a shocking afterword.

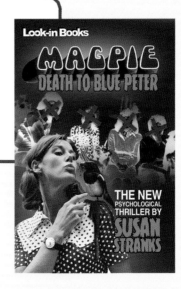

Look-in Books

MAGPIE
DEATH TO BLUE PETER

THE NEW
PSYCHOLOGICAL
THRILLER BY
SUSAN STRANKS

I was right. I said there was something strange about him!

He must be stopped! Millions will be killed if his plan is unleashed... Think of the children!!! We need to infiltrate the next advert!

STEP ABOARD THE JARDIS* FOR EXCITING SPACE THRILLS

* Jigsaws and Relative Dimensions in Space

Celebrate the newest Dr Who with these exclusive jigsaws featuring incredible scenes from the latest TV series!

WHSmith BEST SELLERS

W.H Smith - your leading place for standing around and reading books without having to pay for them.

Sapphire & Steel's Microwave Cookery for Beginners *The time agents turn their hands to the latest in fine dining technology.*

95p

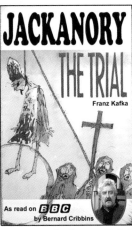

Franz Kafka's The Trial *As seen on 'Jackanory' This special edition features a new introduc--tion by Bernard Cribbins and is illustrated by Quentin Blake.*

85p

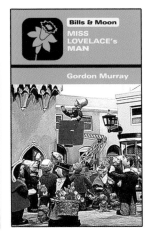

Miss Lovelace's Man *The inhabitants of the sleepy town of Trumpton are shocked when the demure Miss Lovelace returns from holiday married to a 20 year old sailor from Ipswich.*

75p

Doctor Who's Quiz Book of Municipal Refuse Collection Vehicles *Test your knowledge of dust carts with this slim volume of rubbish teasers.*

75p

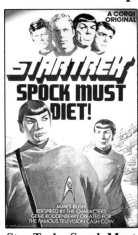

Star Trek - Spock Must Diet *A transporter malfunction creates a duplicate Mr Spock that threatens the safety of Enterprise when he starts to put on weight.*

90p

'Are You Being Served?' Small Business Start-up Guide 1974 *Business mogul Clive Sinclair joins the characters from the popular BBCtv comedy for fun & japes.*

£1.25

Mrs Farrel's CSO Cook Book *Everyone's favourite terrified widow with the odd two dimensional kitchen shares some of her favourite recipes..*

95p

The Ladybird Book of Stockpiling *Get ready for he next global pandemic with this handy guide from the people at Ladybird Books. With some beautiful illustrations.*

75p

For hours of absorbing reading in a warm comfortable environment, choose from thousands of titles at W.H.Smith. Paperbacks, hardbacks, children's books, magazines, comics, periodicals and jazz rags - you'll be able to pick all of them off our shelves and browse through them at you leisure until they are all bent and crumpled ready for the next free-loader to drool over.

WHSMITH   for looking at books and not paying for them

Look-out

RUN! HE'S COMING!!!

Ha ha haaaaa! The plan is working. Soon the wonderful world of Radio One will be mine and soon the wonderful world of the er... world will be mine. I'll control everything from Wally Whyton to The Laughing Policeman and beyond... ... . Hang on, what's this. Who are you? What are you doing to me? Put me down. Unhand me madam. Why are his hands so cold? Nooooooooo!

He's got his back to us. He hasn't seen us. I've managed to squeeze the two of us into this single column unnoticed... **but we're only in black & white!**

It's alright. I've retained my blueness. Now you'll need to pose a question **before** we can act... Once you've done that, you can **trap** him in one of his infernal books!

ASK Sapphire and STEEL

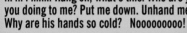

REGINALD BOSANQUET's BEST JOKES EVER
Edited by Peter Haining

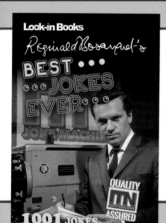

Reggie and his team at ITN - one of the world's funniest news providers - have gathered together some of the **best jokes, gags and spoofs** from their popular comedy show and packed them into **124 pages of mirth**. Discover what happened after the chicken crossed the road with the likes of **Andrew Gardner** and **Alistair Burnett** with additional commentary from correspondents from across the world including **Look-in's own Peter Fairley** - who shows just how funny space can be when you've got a stack of jokes to tell..

There is a threat from a photographic representation of the radio personality Ed "Stewpot" Stewart that has somehow gained sentience and is threatening space/time causality with its plans for world domination. Can you help?

Anon, Chiswick

Sapphire writes: Thank you so much for your charming letter. Please remain calm and Steel and myself with deal with the situation. In the mean time, you must burn every copy of Look-in that has the sentient Stewpot image in it. When I say, 'Every issue', I mean every issue. If only a single one were to survive, then the entity will be able to gain a further foothold on this planet. **Thank you.**

STEWPOT'S INCREDIBLE LSD HALLUCINATIONS
Edited by Sapphire and Steel

"**What's happening??? Where am I?**" "We've trapped you inside the pages of a book - one of the very books you were using to infiltrate reality!" "But... but you can't do this to me. My plans. My power..." "Your plans and your power will not extend beyond the pages of this book!" "**I'll escape and you two meddling time agents will be the first to succumb to my wrath!!**" "We won't... This book has been placed on the island of Krakatoa on a certain date in 1883. You'll be totally destroyed!!" "Nooooo!" +BOOM+

SAPPHIRE & STEEL's MICROWAVE COOKERY
Edited by Chuck Bunnion

"We've done it... but at what cost. We're trapped!!" "Inside a microwave cookbook of all things!" "I saw the future... and it was our future..." "Oh, shut up with your bloody hindsight shit. You've done it again haven't you? Fifteen millenia we spent inside that ruddy transport cafe in space and what did you learn...?? Nothing. And I now have a hatred of playing chess." "Sorry!"

THE END?*

* Yes.

Sapphire and **STEEL**

EXCLUSIVE RANGE

Sapphire and STEEL LOW FAT SPREAD

SAPPHIRE & STEEL
LOW FAT SPREAD
2kg

£3.99

SAPPHIRE and STEEL OATS

Oat So Temporal

FUSTY OLD RAILWAY STATION FLAVOUR
12 sachets

2 MINS
TO ETERNAL IMPRISONMENT IN A HELLISH SHADOW REALM
Just add milk!

SAPPHIRE & STEEL
LOW FAT SPREAD
200g

£1

Sapphire and STEEL LOW FAT SPREAD

only £1

Sapphire and STEEL

SAPPHIRE & STEEL
OATS SO TEMPORAL

£1
Pk of 6

NEW RECIPE

SAPPHIRE and **STEEL**
GOLD CAPPUCCINO

Great NEW taste

8 MUGS

Crafted for trans-dimensional tears in the

Sapphire & Steel™

SIMPLY ADD MILK/ WATER/ REGRET!

Pancake Mix

NEW LOOK!

SAME Great DANGER

OVERLY COMPLICATED SERVING SUGGESTION

SAPPHIRE & STEEL
PANCAKE MIX

£1

Sapphire & STEEL's

Windoclene
FOR GLASS & TRANS-DIMENSIONAL SURFACES

Great NEW taste

ORIGINAL CREAM CLEANER

NO SMEARS! NO MESS!

500ml

SAPPHIRE & STEEL
GOLD CAPPUCCINO
500ml

£1.50

SAPPHIRE & STEEL
WINDO-CLENE
500ml

£2

GREAT VALUE AT A GREAT PRICE!!

I DON'T TRUST IT!

Garmfoods

The Venerable BBC Junior Television Magazine

BEBE

15p

Number 3
February 12th –
18th February 1985

TREVOR EVE'S MOUSTACHE

FREE INSIDE!

THIS INCREDIBLE
YOSSER HUGHES MASK

DEREK JAMESON:
WHY?

THE MAD DEATH

COMIC STRIP action

GONNA KILL EVERY STINKIN' POODLE IN CHISWICK...

START WITH OLD MRS COOT!

Judith Hann's
TOMORROW'S WORLD
DEATH WISH

plus

DOUBLE-SIDED

LIFE AND LOVES OF A SHE DEVIL

POSTER

GREAT NEWS INSIDE READERS!

ON SALE NOW!

CROSSROADS

BATTLES

IN KING'S OAK

4

£2.50
FORTNIGHTLY

"TELL ME YOU LOVE ME!"

DAVID HUNTER SHOT!

48

CROSSROADS
BATTLES IN KING'S OAK

TELL ME YOU LOVE ME!

Players holding the David Hunter card may want to call for an ambulance.

77

CROSSROADS
BATTLES IN KING'S OAK

BEAUTY CONTEST

You've won second prize in a beauty contest. Collect £10 from each player.

89

CROSSROADS
BATTLES IN KING'S OAK

AWKWARD GUEST BONUS CARD

CARRY COT

This card must be surrendered to guests requesting a cot in their chalet. It will be charged at £4.50 per night and a 10% surcharge will be added to their final bill to cover the cost of dry cleaning and pot porri.

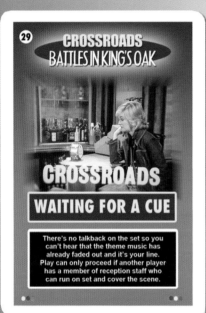

29

CROSSROADS
BATTLES IN KING'S OAK

CROSSROADS

WAITING FOR A CUE

There's no talkback on the set so you can't hear that the theme music has already faded out and it's your line. Play can only proceed if another player has a member of reception staff who can run on set and cover the scene.

62

CROSSROADS
BATTLES IN KING'S OAK

FAKE MEG

The strange man in chalet four steals one of Meg's dresses and spends the next few days impersonating her. He manages to order new curtains for reception and commission the re-decorating of the bar area before he is discovered. Cards featuring motel staff cannot be used for the next round.

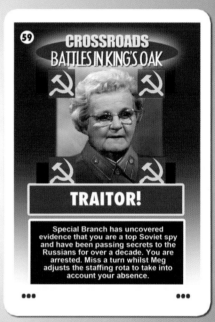

59

CROSSROADS
BATTLES IN KING'S OAK

TRAITOR!

Special Branch has uncovered evidence that you are a top Soviet spy and have been passing secrets to the Russians for over a decade. You are arrested. Miss a turn whilst Meg adjusts the staffing rota to take into account your absence.

24

CROSSROADS
BATTLES IN KING'S OAK

Can you smell something burning?

MOTEL FIRE

All players must surrender any card in their hand that have images of Meg on them. Players may only claim back their Meg cards if, after two rounds, they are in posession of the QE2 card. All other Meg cards will play no further part in the game.

29

CROSSROADS
BATTLES IN KING'S OAK

TOWELS

The family in chalet four have called reception and urgently need more towels. There are none in the store-room. Do the other players have any? Have you checked the airing cupboard upstairs? Hurry!

39

CROSSROADS
BATTLES IN KING'S OAK

CLINIC RESULTS

A telephone call from the clinic gives you the all-clear! Celebrate with a dry sherry in the motel bar. Take a meal card from the player on your left.

40

CROSSROADS
BATTLES IN KING'S OAK

IMPROMPTU SONG

This card can only be played if you hold a JOHNNY PATRICK or a CHESTER HARRIOT card.
All other players must put up with your singing for the next two rounds.

33

CROSSROADS
BATTLES IN KING'S OAK

VOORD IN THE SHOWER

The lady in chalet six is complaining about the Voord in her shower.
Go back three spaces.

33

CROSSROADS
BATTLES IN KING'S OAK

SOUL SEARCHING

Recent events are playing heavy on Meg's mind. Heavier than is normal for a popular West Midlands female businessman... Maybe it's time. The player holding the Meg Mortimer card must write a touching letter of resignation from the game and leave it where no one can find it.

27

CROSSROADS
BATTLES IN KING'S OAK

GREEK PROMOTIONAL TRAILER

The series has been sold to Greece for some reason. Everything must stop for Meg to record a special 'catch-up' trailer as the TV station can't afford to buy the 2999 previous episodes (or doesn't want to).
Play takes a break for an hour. Have a small sherry while you wait.

19

CROSSROADS
BATTLES IN KING'S OAK

GLAMOUR

It's the night of the West Midlands Female Businessman of the Year Awards. You've been tipped off that you have won the top prize and you haven't a thing to wear. You need to nip into town without anyone knowing to do some 'shopping'. If you hold the FAKE MEG card, use it to distract the staff.

30

CROSSROADS
BATTLES IN KING'S OAK

FIRE DAMAGE

Following the motel fire, it's business as usual but a wedding needs to be cancelled as the curtains in the banqueting suite need bleaching. All staff cards cannot be played during the next round as they are busy helping Stan and the builders.

79

CROSSROADS
BATTLES IN KING'S OAK

GOODBYE, JILL!!

QE2

There's a band playing and a force ten gale. You didn't burn in the motel fire after all. You're now happily waving goodbye to your daughter forever... at least until a surprise reunion in Venice...
This card can soften the blow for another player playing the MOTEL FIRE card. You get to keep your dignity... but only just!

20

CROSSROADS
BATTLES IN KING'S OAK

NEW OWNERS

New owners take over the motel and begin to dismantle Meg's legacy. The writing is on the wall. The game will end shortly following five rounds where nothing much happens. Discard all cards featuring motel employees over the age of 40.

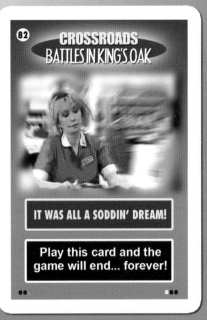

82

CROSSROADS
BATTLES IN KING'S OAK

IT WAS ALL A SODDIN' DREAM!

Play this card and the game will end... forever!

Doctor WHO

The Kandy Man - Evil servant of Helen A - leader
of The Happiness Patrol on the planet Terra Alpha.

ANOTHER ADEQUATE

DOCTOR WHO

FIGURE from

GAYDOLL

THE
ROYAL
COMMEMORA
SERVO
ROBOT

Doctor Who logo ©1996 USS Enterprises

ANOTHER ADEQUATE

DOCTOR WHO

FIGURE from

GAYDOLL

DENYS
FISHER
CYBERMAN

ANOTHER ADEQUATE

DOCTOR WHO

FIGURE from

GAYDOLL

PINK
QUARK

Doctor Who logo ©1996 USS Enterprises

Doctor WHO

The Rani - Evil Timelady scientist and enemy of
The Doctor. She controlled the deadly Tett Traps.

DAPOL

© 1988 BBC Enterprises / Pip & Jane Baker.
Produced under exclusive worldwide licence.

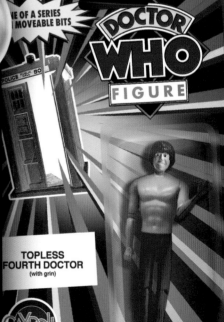

VE OF A SERIES
I MOVEABLE BITS

DOCTOR WHO FIGURE

TOPLESS
FOURTH DOCTOR
(with grin)

GAYDOLL

No. 9 MARCH 26th 2005 SATURDAYS

4p

Jackie

"I'm in my dressing gown...

"There's a strange man in my bedroom...

"Well, anything could happen!"

a hatchet publication

BUILD YOUR OWN
DALEK

Nerry Nahun

BBC
DOCTOR WHO

ISSUE 01

ONLY
£1.99
Regular price £9.99

FULL SIZE
MOVING PARTS
SENTIENT
AND HIGHLY
DANGEROUS!
NOT A TOY

THIS DALEK BELONGS TO JUSTIN

INCLUDES
REAL
GENETIC
MATERIAL*
*Government licence required
for handling and storage

brazed on

8 equally spaced steel rods

brass ring

brass ring

inner tube 275mm

...YOU'LL NEED TO CONSTRUCT
...KILLING MACHINE

£9.99 only £1.99
NOT FOR SALE IN COUNTRIES WHERE LAWS
PREVENT INVASIVE GENETIC EXPERIMENTATION

FORTNIGHTLY
ISSUE 01

FANTASTIC
FIRST ISSUE

MORE ISSUES TO COME!
MANY MORE!!!

NOT A TOY

a hatchet publication

BBC

DOCTOR WHO

ISSUE 01

1 : EYE STALK HOUSING

BUILD YOUR OWN DALEK - Issue 1

Eye Piece base

Eye stalk core

Fenders x6

Eye piece ribbed coupling

Space screws x50

Lens

WHAT'S IN YOUR FIRST THREE ISSUES?

ISSUE 1

Including...
EYE STALK MECHANISM HOUSING
and a bag of screws

Inside the magazine...

- Full instructions for assembling the eye stalk housing
- Genesis of the Daleks - How they began
- Who was Davros - the genius mastermind behing the Daleks
- Genetic splicing - the formation of a credible mutant foetus

ISSUE 2

Including...
LENS & DIGITAL FEEDBACK ENHANCER COIL
and another bag of screws

Inside the magazine...

- Full instructions for assembling the eye stalk neural interface
- The Thals - Innocent peace makers or cruel slave drivers
- The colour of your Dalek - Do's and don't's
- Correct nutrients for healthy mutant foetus development

ISSUE 3

Including...
HOLOGRAPHIC IMAGING INTERFACE
and a further bag of screws

Inside the magazine...

- Full instruction for imaging interface assembly and charging
- The thickness of Dalek fenders since the original mark three
- Do I need a TV licence for my imaging interface and other legal stuff
- Ensuring your Dalek mutant is fully sentient during secondary growth

NOT A TOY

"YOU CAN MAKE A GOOD DALEK!"

...in just 45,221 fortnightly parts!

IN FUTURE ISSUES...

ISSUE 4  KALED GENETIC MATERIAL

ISSUE 5  ATOMIC RADIATION DEFLECTOR

ISSUE 6  WASTE MATTER VALVE

ISSUE 7  STATIC ENERGY RELAY

ISSUE 8  KITCHEN SINK PLUNGER

Members of the Dagneham Men's Knitting Circle are introduced to Dalek Krakk at their annual knit-a-thon and general meeting.

Mrs Enid Betamax and her three Dalek care workers on a shopping spree at Meadowhall in Sheffield shortly before the slaughter began.

Mr Alf Spandex - a meat packer for the Royal Marines - gives Dalek Tarrant's stalk a quick seeing to following a brief *'getting-to-know-you'* session in Bury.

Mrs Lillian Zeg and her latest husband pose for the cameras following their marriage at Catford Methodist Church. The union lasted four hours.

THE ULTIMATE KILLING MACHINE

NOT A TOY

EXTENSIVE DETAILED INSTRUCTIONS AND BLUEPRINTS!

Each week, you will be using the most comprehensive plans ever devised. Each intricate diagram has been **hand-drawn** by our dedicated and hard-working team of **North Korean orphans** at a secret facility just outside international laws under special licence from **Kim Jong-un** himself.

AND DON'T FORGET...

...with **issue five** you will get your first sample of genuine organic **KALED™** cells with which you will be able to begin breeding **your very own Dalek mutant** to your unique and specific special specifications. (Providing you have the correct **UK government licence** for this type of domestic genetic engineering - available from **your local post office**.)

YOU WILL OBEY THE INSTRUCTIONS AT ALL TIMES!

DEAR NEWSAGENT

*Please, please, PLEASE reserve for me .... copy/copies of the **OFFICIAL BUILD-YOUR-OWN DALEK** magazine. I will collect it every Thursday and not allow it to pile up in your stockroom for months on end. I also confirm that I have the relevant **'Radioactive Materials Handling' licence** as specified by UK law. **Thank you so much.***

Name..... Dave Ross ..... Age... ?

Address... Bunker Grove, Hull

Radioactive Materials Handling Licence Number 3

I confirm that I am over 21 and not mad at all

Signed..... ..... Date... Yes

SUBSCRIBE NOW...

...and we'll send you absolutely free this splendid dead SKARAN MAGNEDON sealed in a perspex block together with some special RADIATION GLOVES to handle it with. Isn't that just plain tooty??

A LEADING DOCTOR WRITES...

These are the most comprehensive plans for building a Dalek I have ever seen. You could create an army of them in just 45,221 weeks. In some ways it's monstrous but in others, it's totally compelling. I'm afraid... very afraid! In the wrong hands this could be very dangerous but I am totally assured by the makers that everything is safe and under the correct conditions you can create a Dalek that you can be very proud of.. Very proud of indeed!

Doctor W

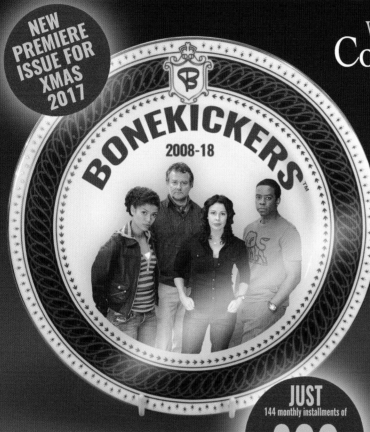

8118055

FREE BUILD YOUR OWN MARTIAN CAPSULE

Bzzzt! Bzzzzzt!!!

Bzzzt! Bzzzzzt!!

BBC

QUATERMASS ADVENTURES

ISSUE 10

COMIC STRIP ACTION

GNAARLL!

WE ARE THE MARTIANS!!

CAROON ATTACKS LITTLE GIRL...

PLUS EXCLUSIVE Cec Linder MEGA POSTER

INSPECTOR LOMAX INVESTIGATES

CAN YOU FOLLOW HIS CLUES?

IT'S DUNCAN LAMONT!

MAKE YOUR OWN MUTANT MONSTER!

COLONEL BREEN'S TOP TEN BOMBS!

panini magazines

ISSUE 10 • 7 JAN.–3 FEB. 2016 • £3.99

10>

9 771750 171074

PLUS!

POSTERS • COMICS • ROCKETS

BBC

VICTOR CARGON'S CONUNDRUMS

AS I'M BEING DEVOURED BY A VEGETABLE-BASED GESTALT ORGANISM, I SPEND A LOT OF TIME SOLVING PUZZLES... IT KEEPS THE HUMAN SIDE OF MY MIND ACTIVE!!

A HAIRY PROBLEM!

A B C

D E

The American Quatermass was visiting Winnerton Flats when his wig blew away again. He's found it but it's got mixed up with some other ones. Can you help him find it before he shouts at you?

WHO'S WHO?

Here's two pics of Professor Quatermass. How many differences can you spot between them?

Colonel Breen's Bomb Bonanza

The Prof's chum Colonel Breen has mislaid his collection of bombs. Can you help him to find all ten of them in this WORD SEARCH before his bosses at the ministry find out?

TNT   FUSION
DIRTY   TIME
ATOM   NUKE
MINE   SCUD
CLUSTER DUD

S	T	E	K	U	N	T
E	N	D	U	R	O	D
N	T	I	M	E	I	U
I	W	R	E	V	S	D
M	O	T	A	D	U	R
S	X	Y	B	C	F	O
R	E	T	S	U	L	C

Answers on page 187

LOST!!

Professor Q is searching for his granddaughter. He needs her help to detonate a nuclear bomb that will destroy the alien menace that is harvesting the youth of the world for food. She's hiding on one of the pages of this comic. Can you find her before the professor? He'd be most grateful!

BRITISH ROCKET GROUP REPORT

ALIEN INDENTIFICATION
Name: MARTIAN

ALIEN TYPE:
Tripodal insectoid

HOME PLANET:
Mars

FUNCTION:
Rocket pilot

AGE:
The Martians crashed their spaceship on Earth FIVE MILLION YEARS AGO!

CRIKEY! THAT'S ANCIENT!!

THREE LEGS:
Enables extra bounce on low gravity planets.

MISSION:
With Mars a dying planet, the inhabitants tried to survive the castastrophe by embedding their DNA in early man. And they would've got away with it if it wasn't for the clever professor and his scientist chums.

TWO EYES:
Both made from condoms.

TWO CLAWS:
For holding things.

LOCATION:
Discovered during building work at Hobb's Lane in LONDON.

ABDOMEN:
Layers of puff pastry moist--end with honey and fresh orange zest.

HOBB'S LANE

PROF. Q says

THESE CREATURES ARE DIABOLICAL ENTITIES FROM PREHISTORIC MARS! I GIVE THEM A FEAR RATING OF FIVE HOMINID SKULLS!!

HOMINID FACTOR

Hobb's Lane is an UNDERGROUND station where trains run through tubular tunnels. Passengers pay money to arrive at their destinations late and angry. It was built in the olden days by Victorian workmen.

THE QUATERMASS DIARIES

Professor Quatermass has had many fantastical adventures over the years – four, actually. He's kept a detailed diary of each of these scientific escapades and has decided to share them with readers of QUATERMASS ADVENTURES. This issue sees the start of his second operation – a tale of alien invasion with the unusual codename – QUATERMASS 2.

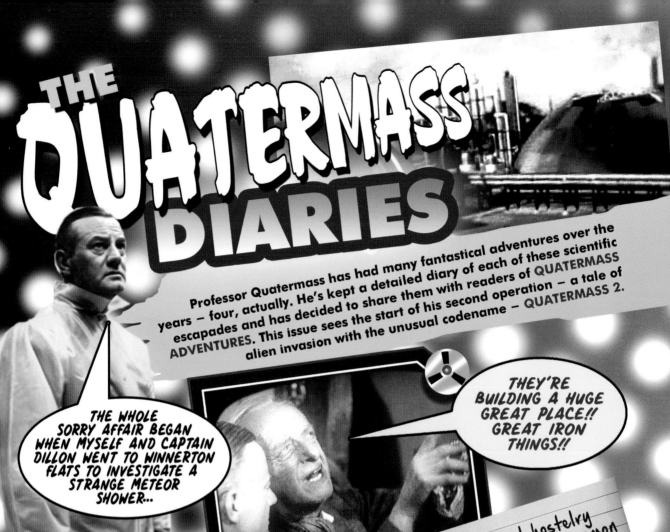

THE WHOLE SORRY AFFAIR BEGAN WHEN MYSELF AND CAPTAIN DILLON WENT TO WINNERTON FLATS TO INVESTIGATE A STRANGE METEOR SHOWER...

THEY'RE BUILDING A HUGE GREAT PLACE!! GREAT IRON THINGS!!

IT'S THE MOON PROJECT... HERE... ON EARTH!!

We nipped into a local hostelry for a quick drink where a common fellow told us of a vast recently built establishment and how it had benefited the locals...

Farppp!!

Despite conning us out of a further round of drinks, the man was right. We saw the buildings from our car and drove nearer to investigate. It all looked very familiar... like the designs for my moonbase. I knew I should've registered them with the patent office...

Nearby we found an intact meteorite. As we approached it, the shell split open and let out a foul smelling blast of gas which overcame the normally stoic Dillon.

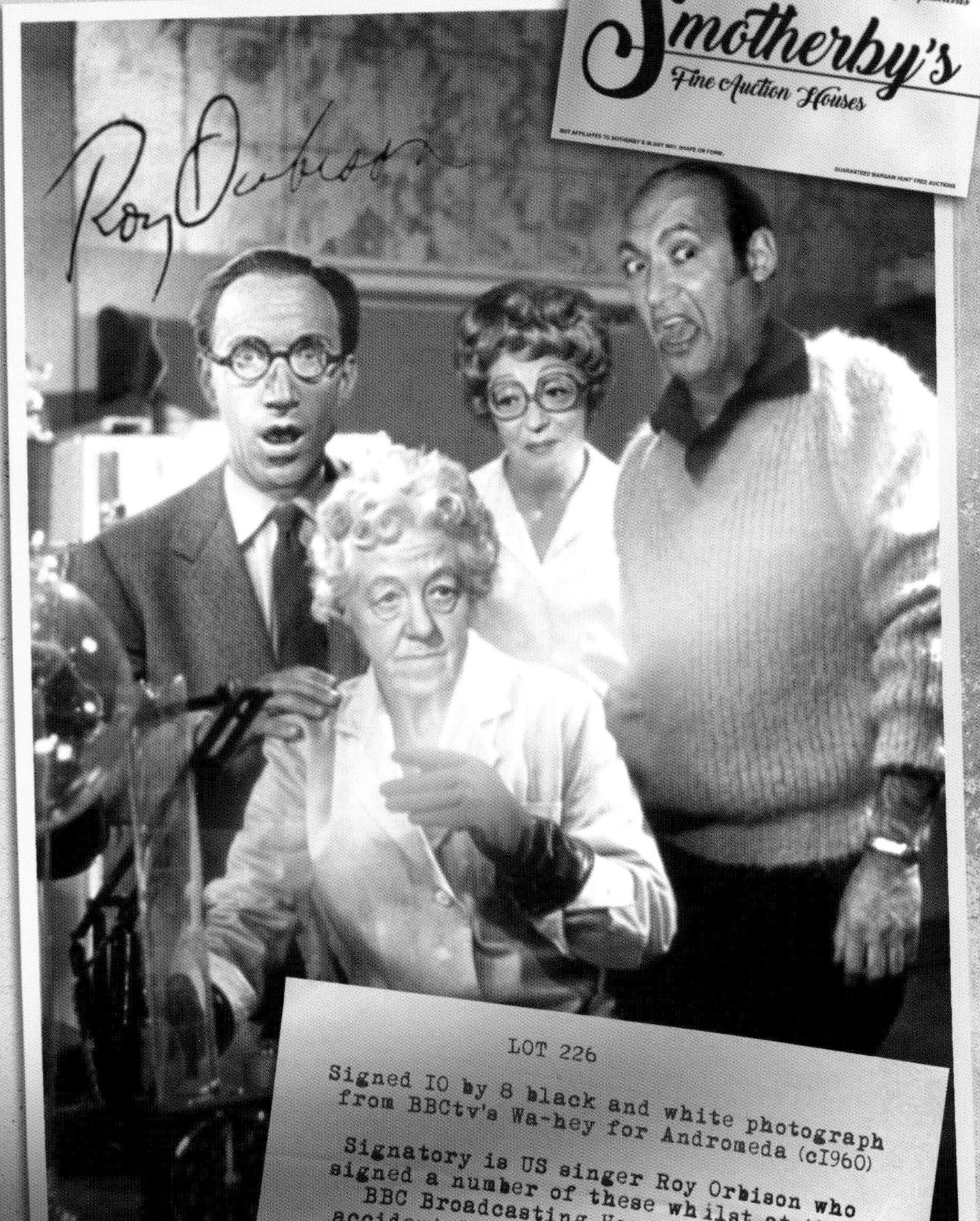

Roy Orbison

LOT 226

Signed IO by 8 black and white photograph
from BBCtv's Wa-hey for Andromeda (cI960)
Signatory is US singer Roy Orbison who
signed a number of these whilst at the
BBC Broadcasting House after being
accidentally given one hundred of them
during a live performance in the radio
studio. It was thought that none survived
and this rare one has been authenticated
by his office.

The best prices for kids at Christmas!

FAYS
Britain's favourite catalogue
Winter/Summer

CHRISTMAS GIFTS

1 **Endeavour Annual** Exciting stories and puzzles featuring the famous junior detective in the interesting town of Oxford.

| CWR.5772 | 75p |

2 **Vigil Annual** Undersea detective tales from the BBCtv series in a book packed with pin-ups, puzzles and oceanic facts.

| VGFH.3664 | 70p |

3 **Van Der Valk Annual** This annual has about as much to do with the TV series as the TV series has with the 70s original.

| TWY.4420 | 70p |

4 **The Pact Annual** More fun and hi-jinx with the staff of the family brewery as they try to cover more murders.

| GSW. 2874 | 70p |

5 **Death in Paradise Annual** Lots of murders at the popular holiday destination. Flights, hotel reservations and tax included.

| COD. 9221 | 70p |

6 **Vigil Annual** Another book featuring the submariner detective due to an error in issuing the licence to produce one.

| TOD. 6298 | 70p |

7 **Vera Annual** Stories, pin-ups and puzzles for a Sunday evening in with the miserable old detective from Northumberland.

| GSR. 2887 | 75p |

8 **Line of Duty Annual** Exciting stories of crime, corruption and betrayal for boys and girls everywhere. Identity of 'H' not included.

| SUS. 2422 | 75p |

9 **Pilkington's Patch Annual** Spin-off TV show featuring the young PC who's the scourge of bent bastards everywhere.

| SUS. 2423 | 75p |

10 **It's A Sin Annual** Join the happy gang at the Pink Palace for fun & games along with stories, pin-ups & features.

| PRF. 9214 | 70p |

11 **Holby City Annual** Stories and features from the successful TV series based in a hospital above a secret military base.

| VDF. 4487 | 75p |

12 **Casualty Annual** Join the doctors and nurses of the BBCtv series for stories and features about gory things.

| JPG. 2003 | 75p |

FAYS
CATALOGUE

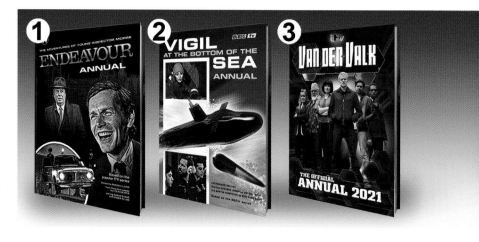

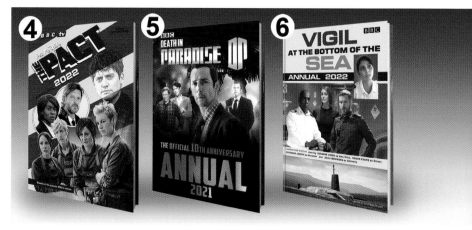

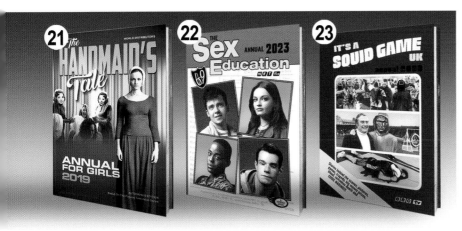

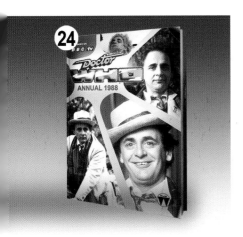

16 Juliet Bravo Annual 96 pages of exciting picture stories plus hints on cooking, sewing, beauty and petty crime.

JWR. 8115	70p

17 London Spy Annual 124 pages of disturbing imagery concerning the dark side of modern espionage and a crossword.

DOA. 4582	80p

18 Cuffs Annual Great stories of crime from the Brighton police. This book will probably help you remember the TV show.

THT. 2318	70p

19 Dominic Littlewood Annual featuring that wacky-zany TV character and his many friends and their colourful lives.

GSR. 1087	75p

20 Hard Sun Annual If you remember this high-concept sci-fi crime drama, then this is the book for you, you poor sod!

HTO. 9836	70p

21 The Handmaid's Tale Annual for girls. Full of puzzles, games, quizzes and stories of feminine woe.

FME. 4747	75p

22 Sex Education Annual Beautifully illustrated stories, picture strips and diagrams from the popular Netflix series.

STD. 3345	85p

23 Squid Game UK Annual Based on the British version of the world-wide hit series - with Stuart Hall & Eddie Waring.

IAK. 8055	75p

24 Doctor Who Annual Stories and features written and illustrated by someone who's never heard of the show.

HFG. 1132	75p

13 Midsomer Murders Annual Packed with Inspector Barnaby's intriguing cases plus pages of jokes, riddles and puzzles.

PNG. 3203	75p

14 EastEnders Annual Those unfriendly cockney folk from Walford in 80 pages of entertainment for kids of all ages.

BGU. 5083	70p

15 Mrs Hudson Adventures Annual The fascinating character from TV's Sherlock in stripped stories to enthral.

JWR. 8115	70p

FAYS
CATALOGUE
Great gifts you'll still be paying for in the afterlife.

25 **A Very English Scandal Annual** Join Norman, Jeremy and Rinka the dog for more hilarious adventures across the UK.

| AMT.2365 | 75p |

26 **Bodyguard Annual** Fun with *The Bodyguard* as he takes on Sooty, Hector's House, Parsley the Lion and Trumpton.

| HGXX.1383 | 70p |

27 **Threads Annual** This annual could save your life. Puzzles and trivia for life in your fall-out shelter. Can also be burned for fuel.

| TWWG.3622 | 70p |

28 **TV Action Annual** All your TV favourites in one book including Dr Who, Hawaii-Five-0 Call the Midwife and Robert Peston.

| GSW. 2874 | 70p |

29 **Crossroads Annual** Motel mayhem with the Queen of the Midlands. Based on the popular drama based on the popular soap.

| DSA. 6273 | 70p |

30 **Balding Annual** She's a mean woman with a mean temper. Crime has no chance. Includes stories, puzzles and roll-up ideas.

| KFD. 9983 | 80p |

31 **Ghosts Annual** Titters & giggles with the spooks of Button Hall with jokes, stories, quizzes and genuine DIY exorcism text.

| BXV. 3640 | 75p |

32 **Agents of SHIELD Annual** Comic book exploits of the TV superhero team that Marvel seem to forget after the 2nd series.

| MAR. 2433 | 75p |

33 **Pointless Annual** The fun adventures of Alexander and Richard. 80 large pages full of information that will be useless in real life.

| SDG. 4532 | 75p |

34 **Years & Years Annual** 124 pages of disturbing predictions for boys and girls everywhere.

| BRS. 3658 | 70p |

35 **Covid 19 Annual** features many of the hilarious cartoon characters from the British Cabinet and their fun affairs.

| SDF. 3882 | 75p |

36 **Rip-Off Britain Annual** A feast of fun with the zany humour of Julia, Gloria and Angela with strip stories and legal action.

| DWH. 5534 | 75p |

FAYS
CATALOGUE

Great gifts dumped outside your front door whilst you are out!

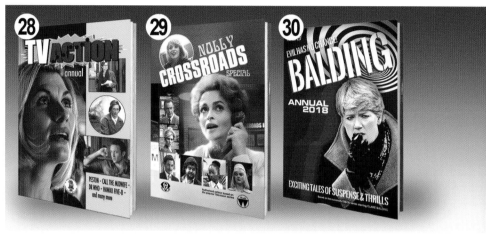

All-New

TIMELORD
Jamboree Special

POLICE BOX

1 234567 890128

UK - £4.99
EUROPE - €1.25

DOCTORS - MONSTERS - VILLAINS - SPACE
ASSISTANTS - ACTORS - TIME MACHINES -
MUTANTS - Err - WORDS - PICTURES - STUFF

100% Unofficial 100% Unwarranted

Welcome to your souvenir fanzine celebrating the departure of the latest Timelord incarnation. We have not only and amazing "who's who" guide to all who have played the nation's favourite Doctor but also feature some of the most popular assistants and most noteworthy monsters.

Don't forget to turn over for your FREE super-sized poster! You can do this by taking this side of the poster in both hands and flipping it so's that the reverse side is showing. That's the side without the writing on!

THE TIME TRAVELLING TIMELORD FROM ANOTHER TIME

DOCTOR WHO is one of the most popular television series in the world. There was even a blockbuster movie in 1996 starring ERIC ROBERTS in the 90s. It's been running on the British televison network since the sixties and has seen many actors take on the role before he was a woman played by an actress. If you're fan of DOCTOR WHO, then people will call you a WHOVIAN but you can call the police and report them for cultural harrassment.

TIME SHIP POLICE BOX

Dr Who travels through the universe in a time machine called 'TARDIS'. Each of the letters in 'TARDIS' stand for another word. This is called an acronym. These are used when terms formed from a collection of words are abbreviated into a single word using the first letter of each word in the original term. Acronymy, like retronymy, is a linguistic process that has existed throughout history but for which there was little to no naming, conscious attention, or systematic analysis until relatively recent times. Like retronymy, it became much more common in the 20th century than it had formerly been.

dr whose who?

There has being lots of different Dr Whos - even a woman one! Here's your complete guide to all of them.

The very first Dr. Who was played as a very old man in 1963 by an legitimate actor called WILLIAM HARTNELL who was a famour celebrity at the time thanks to playing an army sergeant in the classic Dad's Army. He also played the role in the first Carry On film entitled Carry on Nurse. He had to leave when he became too old to play it.

When the very first Dr. Who was killed by Mondasian Cybermen. The role was taken over by the film actor PATRICK TROUGHTON - who was famous for such roles in blockbuster films like The Omen, Sindbad and the Eye of the Tiger and The Cigars of Dracula. He played the part like a tramp and the studio had to be fumigated after every episode.

The third Dr Who was played by the comedian JON PERTWEE. Pertwee was one of the original Goons on The Goon Lark on BBC Radio and appeared in dozens of Carry On films. Playing the role of Dr Who was a huge departure for the funny man as it was a serious role that he took very seriously. He wore filly shirts and a cloak.

TOM BAKER was the most famous Dr Who and appeared on TV screen as the Timelord for most of the 70s. He was also a very successful voice-over artiste having lent his talents to such products as John West tinned salmon, Toilet Duck and Symphony Fitted Kitchens. He also used to be a monk.His Dr Who wore a long hat and a floppy scarf.

PAUL DAVISON was studying to become a vet when he was chosen to play the youngest Dr Who. Before that he had appeared almost naked in the 70s soft porn movie 'A Man for Emily'. He played the man. Like his Dr Who, he loved cricket and had once played a game of it. He's also the only Dr Who to be his own father-in-law.

COLIN BAKER was originally one of The Brothers and became the sixth Dr Who when he was booked as the entertainment for the wedding of the show's producer. He'd been in the series before but was sacked after he accidentally shot the lead actor. He went on to present a series of 'I'm A Celebrity Get Me Out Of Here!' but was voted out at the next general election.

THE MASTERS

Every hero needs a super villain and Dr.WHO's villain is one of the most super. He's called THE MASTER and has been played by many actors over the years - including like Dr.WHO, a woman one! Fancy!!! The first Master was ROGER DELGADO who was once the Spanish Ambassador to Britain before taking up acting. The next major Master was TONY AINLEY who wore a special wig to look a lot more like the character. In the American movie version of the series, the Master was played by Hollywood star ERIC ROBERTS who was famous as the brother of Welsh actress Rachel Roberts. When the series returned in 2005, Martian actor JOHN SIM took on the role before becoming a woman played by MICHAEL GOMEZ. She is currently being played by SACHA DISTEL from The History Boys.

Children's entertainer SYLVESTER McCOY got the role following an audition where he had to portray how Dr Who would react to having a ferret stuck down his trousers. There was a huge question mark over whether his Dr Who should carry an umbrella. Since leaving the role, he ended up in New Zealand where he claims he was making a Hollywood movie.

PAUL McGANN played an American Dr Who who kissed another doctor in a TV movie pilot made by Stephen Spielberg. Although a full series wasn't made, he continued to play the role anyway until his adventures finally turned up on CD. He's still at it. He is also one of the famous McGann brothers who include Joe, Stephen and Renault.

CHRISTOPHER ECCLESTONE became the ninth Dr Who when the show returned to television screens in 2004. He'd previously been known as a northen actor with appearances in 'Christmas Cracker' - a special festive episode of the popular Robbie Coltrane police series and the quiz show 'Let Them Have It'. Despite spending only a year as Dr Who, he is still remembered.

DAVID TENNANT played the tenth new Dr Who and became the very second actor to portray the Timelord in the new series. He had been a Casanova for show-runner Russell T Davies and this had impressed the writer. Since leaving the show, he has found fame in the ITV drama 'Broadchurch' which he took to the US and failed with. He then played the young Michael Palin in the sequel to 'Around the World in Eighty Days'.

MATT SMITH's grandparents were only teenagers when Dr Who began on BBCtv in 1963. They had no idea that their then unborn grandson would be playing the elderly Timelord in the future present day of 2010. Matt was a former sports reporter for ITV when it was announced he would be the youngest eleventh Dr Who ever. He recently appeared in 'Terminator: JennySiss'.

PETER CAPALDI is the only Dr Who to have won an Oscar™. Sadly it wasn't for playing the Timelord in a big Hollywood blockbuster movie. He had been a fan of the series since it began and had made it his life-long ambition to play the part when he wrote to the Radio Times demanding the sacking of Robert Holmes for his portrayal of the Time Lords in the Dr WHO episode, 'The Deadly Assassin'.

JODY WHITTAKER is the latest woman actor to play the role of Dr WHO. She is also the first female. New producer Chris Chinball first met Jody on the set of 'Broadchurch - an ITV drama that sadly only lasted three seasons. He was so impressed by her Yorkshire-ness that he had no hesitation at casting her as the 13th Dr Who. She is currently leaving the show following a worldwide pandemic.

The OTHER Dr WHOS

Lots of other people have played Dr WHO too! The horror actor PETER CUSHING played him in two blockbuster movies in the 60s. LORD JOHN HURT was the War Dr Who in a special episode to celebrate Matt Smith's 50th birthday. Hurt's catchphrase was "I'm not a human being - I'm a Timelord!" There's also been comedian ROWAN ATKINSON who appeared in a sitcom version of the series. He won the role in a charity raffle for Comic's Relief with the runners up (including HUGH GRANT and JOANNA LUMLEY) having small roles in the episode. RICHARD E. GRANT was a cartoon Dr Who but not many people saw him as it was on the internet only.

Dr WHO's AMAZING ASSISTANTS

Dr WHO has had loads of assistants over the years. From schoolgirls to university professors and from mathematical boys in pyjamas to northen comedians. He's had them all. Here are some of the most memorable. How many are you able to remember?

MANDIP GILL as Yaz
She was a young woman police-man when she first met Dr Who. She didn't tell Dr Who something just before she left. She was named after a banana milk drink.

BRADLEY WALSH as Graeme
A former London bus driver and stepfather to Tosin. he first appeared in 'The Chase'.

FRAZER HINES as Joe Sugden
Joe left Emmerdale to spend time with his mother Annie in Spain. It wasn't long before news reached the village that he had been killed in a road accident.

LOUISE JAMESON as Leyla
Leyla was a savage woman from an alien planet whom Dr Who met when he turned up to fix her race's PC. She eventually fell in love with a Timelord policeman following a brief chat.

CAROLINE JOHN as Liz Shaw
Liz was an incredibly intelligent scientist from Cambridge Univ--ersity and although she only appeared in the series for a year. she was still pretty good.

LOUISE JENNA COLEMAN as Clara
Clara was better known as the Improbable Woman after she rescued Dr Who by retconing all his previous adventures for his anniversary. She was killed by an angry bird but came back a few times.

ARTHUR DARVILL as Rory Stewart
Rory Stewart OBE is an academic, diplomat, explorer, author, former soldier, and former Secretary of State for International Development. He is 49.

LEELA WARD as Romana 2
When the first Romana changed her appearance, she ended up looking like this. She eventually married Dr Who for a year following her purchase of a Prime computer.

ROSS KEMP as Grant
First met Dr Who in an episode entitled 'Dimensions in Time' where he and his brother helped Romana escape from the Rani.

WILLIAM RUSSELL, JACQUELINE HILL and CAROLE ANN FORD as Ian, Barbara and Susan
This trio were Dr Who's first assistants. Ian and Barbara were schoolteachers and Susan was really Dr Who's actual granddaughter who stole the TARDIS with him.

A MASSIVE MENAGERIE OF MENACING MONSTERS

Dr WHO has met many terrifying monsters both in front of and behind the camera. From deadly Dodos to minging Maggots, Dr WHO has met them all! We've sifted through the Timelord's many files to dig out the most notorious and most dangerous creatures from all the corners of the galaxy. Here are some of the most frightening...

DALEKS
The evil creatures in the Whooniverse. They were created by Davros on the planet Skaro following a neutron war which mutated the Kaled race. Daleks have been bred to hate all other lifeforms and will stop at nothing to become rulers of the solar system. They can now also climb stairs.

THE MANDRILLS
Giant hulking monsters from the planet Eden. They were captured by Professor Tryst who planned to use them to make drugs. He was thwarted when he crashed his spaceship into the TARDIS.

THE CYBER MEN
Centuries ago by our Earth time, the people of the planet Telos dreamed of eternal life and created artificial replacements for their limbs and organs - until eventually they'd even replaced their brains with computers. So the Cyber Men were born.

TARAN WOOD BEAST
A fierce wild creature that lives in the forests of the planet Tara. One attacked the Doctor's assistant Romany but she was rescued by the local Count who thought she looked like his princess.

THE PLASMATONS
Strange grey blobby monsters created by the Master to capture Concorde which was a famous aeroplane in the 1980s. The Doctor had to travel to prehistoric Earth to defeat them!

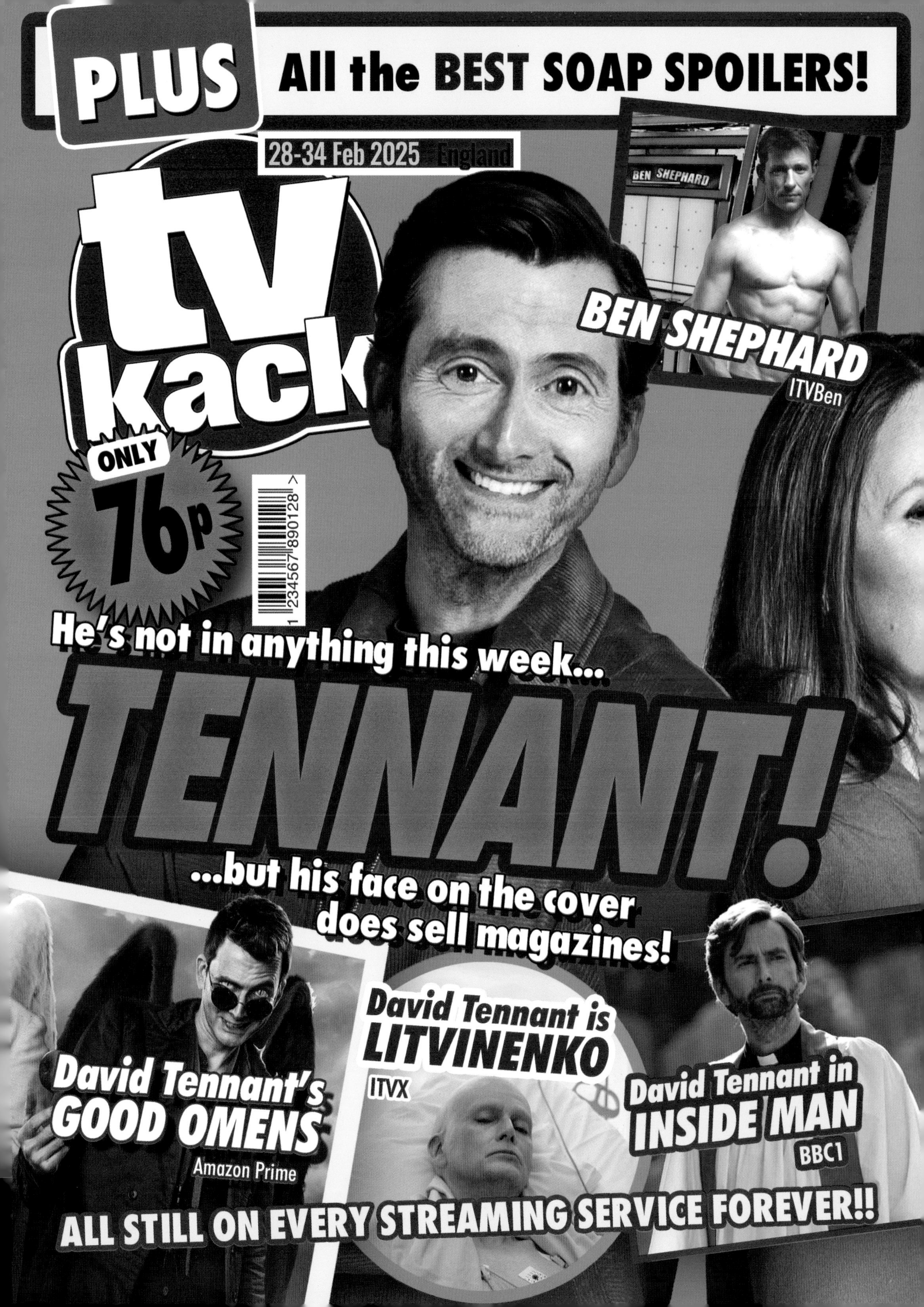
PLUS
All the BEST SOAP SPOILERS!
28-34 Feb 2025 England
tv kack
ONLY
76p
1 234567 890128 >
BEN SHEPHARD
BEN SHEPHARD
ITVBen
He's not in anything this week...
TENNANT!
...but his face on the cover does sell magazines!
David Tennant's GOOD OMENS
Amazon Prime
David Tennant is LITVINENKO
ITVX
David Tennant in INSIDE MAN
BBC1
ALL STILL ON EVERY STREAMING SERVICE FOREVER!!

TV KACK – IT'S YOUR NUMBER ONE READ WHILST HAVING A LONG GOOD DUMP!

BBC1

2.15pm - Mark Williams isn't feeling himself in Father Brown.

6am Breakfast Two fried eggs, bacon, sausage, beans, tomatoes, mushrooms, fried bread and tea or coffee £6.95

9.15 Morning Wood with *Gethin Jones*

10.0 You're in Great Danger! *Rav Wilding* explains to the elderly that there's nothing they can do to prevent scam artists and home invasions with violent dramatic reconstructions and first hand testimony from former victims. (1/5)

10.45 Benefit Fraud Scum with Alex Jones. The popular One Show presenter joins Catford police as they stalk and arrest a forty-two year old mother of three who failed to declare to the authorities the £10 cash she received for doing a dress alteration for a neighbour. (6/20)

11.15 Homes Under the Hammer Property porn with *Martin Daniels, Dionne Warwick* and the other one. The trio visit houses in Brighton and St. Albans and a disused public toilet in Derby. (450,342/10,000,000) (Rpt)

12.15pm Bargain Hunt Today's show comes from the Aldi Superstore on Winton Road in Allcester where the Reds and the Blues have an hour to find three items in the middle isle to take to auction on eBay. The winner gets food for the week. (Rpt)

1.0 News for One with *Dame Rula Lenska*. Budget news for people living on their own. *Followed by weather for ducks.*

1.45 Doctors Only urgent appointments. *Your call is seventh in the queue and will be answered shortly.*

2.15 Father Brown *Sins of the Father* The jovial Catholic priest find himself under suspicion when the local abortion clinic is torched. (6/10) (Rpt)

3.0 Escape to Another Country *Alistair Appleton* assists another desperate English couple in their plans to make a better life in a country other than the UK before they are discovered by the authorities. (Rpt)

4.0 The Repair Shop Visitors to the barn bring in the Economy, the Rail Network and the NHS for repair after years of neglect.

5.15 Pointless Isn't everything? (Rpt)

BBC2

7.30pm - Martin Fowler's love affair is discovered by Stacey in EastEnders.

6.0pm The Five O'Clock News *Read by Dick & Dom.* (Viewers in Wales get the programmes they deserve.)

6.30 Local News All your the local news in a single nationally transmitted bulletin. *Read by Rylan*

7.0 The One Show *Alex Jones* and a former boyband member who now needs to feed his wife and kids are joined by several guests, some of whom will be allowed to say something interesting before being told to shut up for an eight minute segment about the plight of song thrushes in the Outer Hebrides. *(Also available as a sedative from your local GP and horse doctor.)*

7.30 EastEnders Whilst digging in the Vic's cellar, Sonia uncover ancient documents that prove Walford is legally part of France.

8.0 A Question of Sport *A question of why?*

8.30 Would I Lie To You? *Rob Brydon* and team captains *David Mitchell* and *Lee Mack* are joined by *Boris Johnson, Dominic Raab, Matt Hancock* and *Nadine Dorres* for more lying and getting away with it. (Rpt)

9.0 Kill the Midwife *Sins of the Father - Part One* A slaughter at Nonnatus House and Sister Julienne (*Jenny Agutter*) is concerned that the nun's midwifery service is at risk. (9/10) (Rpt)

10.0 Ten O'Clock News Read by *Scarlett Moffatt* and *Joey Essex*

10.40 Disney's Question Time Presented by *Donald Duck* Guests include Buzz Lightyear (Con), Captain Nemo (Green), Herbie (Lib) and Dumbo (Lab).

10.40 The Whatever-Was-On-BBC3--Over-The-Weekend Show *Stacey Dooley* presents whatever was on BBC3 over the weekend in this rather shameless attempt to fill the schedules with alleged "new content" that's actually cheaper than showing re-runs of *Silent Witness* and *Mrs Brown's Boys*. **12.0am Closedown**

BBC2

11.25am - The Emley Moor transmitter tower has problems in today's report.

6.0am - 11.0 Teleshopping

11.0 Play School It's Monday! *with Huw Edwards and Clive Myrie* (Rpt)

11.25 Transmitter Information

11.30 Colour Film The Homemade Car

11.55 - 11.59pm Teleshopping

12.00am Closedown

ITV1

3.0pm - Adil Ray has all the right answers in today's Cunning Lingo.

6.0am Good Morning Britain News

9.0 Lorraine Chat show **10.0 This Morning** Lifestyle and shallow fluff

12.30pm Loose Women Ignorant opinion

1.30 Lunchtime News Current affairs

2.0 Dickhead's Real Scam Have you got a valuable object you want to sell but don't know it's real value. Then we have some scam artists are very interested in hearing from you...

3.0 Cunning Lingo Dirty word game

4.0 Tipping Point *Ben Shephard* hosts the quiz in which contestants answer general knowledge questions to win turns on a giant *Penny Drop* arcade machine. They drop tokens down a choice of four chutes - each with pegs to render the token's journey irratic. When it lands flat, the moving base pushes it into further tokens which may or may not fall onto a further moving base. If they are lucky, then tokens will possibly fall into a tray below. Contestants get £50 for each token that is captured in the tray. Sometimes a token with a question mark falls and this means the lucky contestant wins a prize like a spa weekend or tickets to a theme park or a hamper of cheeses. The players who win the least amount are ejected after each round until the last player goes forward into the final to win a possible £10,000 if they manage to get a slightly larger token through the machine and out again. If not, they just win what they've earned. If they can drop the special token along with a "X2" marked token, then their prize is doubled to £20,000 (though this rule wasn't added until recently and may not feature in repeats). If the final round is good, it will end up in a schedule filler series entitled *'Tipping Point's Greatest Finals'*

5.0 The Chase Quiz

6.0 Regional News News programme

6.30 ITV Evening News News programme

7.30 Emmerdale Soap

8.0 Coronation Street Soap

9.0 Nolly (1/3) Drama about a soap.

10.0 ITV News/Weather News about soaps followed by soap weather programme.

10.30 Regional News/Weather News programme followed by weather programme.

10.45 Peston Repeat of Sunday morning's edition for viewers who had a lie in. (Rpt)

11.15 Catchphrase Stephen Mulhern sentences three more members of the public to purgatory. (Rpt)

12.0am Teleshopping

ITV2

5.30pm - Harry Hill returns with more video clips in You've Been Framed

6am You've Been Framed (Rpt)
6.30 You've Been Framed (Rpt) **7.0** You've Been Framed (Rpt) **7.30** You've Been Framed (Rpt) **8.0** You've Been Framed (Rpt) **8.30** You've Been Framed (Rpt) **9.0** You've Been Framed (Rpt) **9.30** You've Been Framed (Rpt) **10.0** You've Been Framed (Rpt) **10.30** You've Been Framed (Rpt) **11.0** You've Been Framed (Rpt) **11.30** You've Been Framed (Rpt)

12.00 pm You've Been Framed *More candid home video hi-jinks with Harry Hill.* (Rpt) **12.30** You've Been Framed *Join Harry for some more camcorder mishaps* (Rpt) **1.0** You've Been Framed *Presented by Harry Hill* (Rpt) **1.30** You've Been Framed *A collection of some of the best video disasters sent in by viewers.* (Rpt). **2.0** You've Been Framed *Harry Hill narrates more funny videos.* (Rpt) **2.30** You've Been Framed *Join Harry and the gang for more hilarious japes captured on video.* (Rpt) **3.0** You've Been Framed *with Harry Hill* (Rpt) **3.30** You've Been Framed *Video mishaps* (Rpt) **4.0** You've Been Framed *Harry Hill is back with more of your antics caught on tape.* (Rpt) **4.30** You've Been Framed *As 11.30am* **5.0** You've Been Framed *More surprises from Harry Hill* (Rpt) **5.30** You've Been Framed *Another dig into the vault of mishaps with Harry Hill.* (Rpt)

6.0pm You've Been Framed Special *featuring the very best of the series with Harry Hill.* (Rpt)

7.0 You've Been Framed *Harry Hill unleashes more laughter with a further selection of wacky clips from the YBF archive.* (Rpt)

8.0 You've Been Framed's Greatest Hits: 4 *The fourth installment of the best funny mishaps specially chosen by Harry Hill's production team.* (Rpt)

9.0 You've Been Framed *More surprises from Harry Hill* (Rpt)

10.0 You've Been Framed *Harry Hill is finally captured and put on trial in this special two-hour season finale.*

12.0am You've Been Framed (Rpt)

12.30 You've Been Framed (Rpt) **1.0** You've Been Framed **1.30** You've Been Framed (Rpt) **2.0** You've Been Framed (Rpt) **2.30** You've Been Framed (Rpt) **3.0** You've Been Framed (Rpt) **3.30** You've Been Framed (Rpt) **4.0** You've Been Framed (Rpt) **5.30** You've Been Framed (Rpt)

ITV3

5.15pm - It's murder for DCI Tom Barnaby in Midsomer Murders

6am Midsomer Murders (Rpt)
7.0 Midsomer Murders (Rpt) **8.10** Midsomer Murders (Rpt) **9.15** Midsomer Murders (Rpt) **10.15** Midsomer Murders (Rpt) **11.15** Midsomer Murders (Rpt)

12.30 pm Midsomer Murders *with John Nettles as Detective Chief Inspector Barnaby who investigates a serious murder in this episode of the popular crime drama.* (Rpt) **1.45** Midsomer Murders *A body has been found and the DCI finds himself looking into another murder case in the picturesque county.* (Rpt) **3.0** Midsomer Murders *A deadly case of murder confounds Barnaby in the county of Midsomer.* (Rpt)

4.05 Midsomer Murders *A murderer is sought when a corpse is discovered. Stars John Nettles as Detective Chief Inspector Barnaby.* (Rpt)

5.15 Midsomer Murders *The green lawns of Midsomer are stained red with blood when a body is discovered and DCI Barnaby (John Nettles) finds himself hunting down a murderer in this episode of the long-running crime drama.* (Rpt)

6.25 Midsomer Murders *Tom Barnaby is called in when a dead person is discovered and it seems to have been murdered. With John Nettles.* (Rpt)

7.50 Midsomer Murders *A murder has been committed on a body in the county of Midsomer and the corpse is looked into by DCI Barnaby* (Rpt)

9.00 Midsomer Murders *The body is dead and the stench of murder hangs heavy across the county of Midsomer as Detective Chief Constable Tom Barnaby is dealt another case.* (Rpt)

10.15 Midsomer Murders *Following a complaint from a member of the public, the PCC suspends the Midsomer County Police Force in order to investigate claims that the county's murder rate is at least thirty times higher than any other in the UK. (Not including Scotland)* (Rpt)

ITV4

11.0am - Another case for Number Six in The Prisoner

6am The Prisoner *Do Not Forsake Me Oh My Darling Espionage series starring Nigel Stock* (Rpt) **7.0** The Prisoner *Dance of the Dead Light entertainment show. Presented by Mary Morris* (Rpt) **8.0** The Prisoner *Many Happy Returns with Patrick McGoohan as a secret agent man who becomes trapped in a North Wales village.* (Rpt) **9.0** The Prisoner *Free for All Patrick McGoohan as secret agent six becomes involved in politics.* (Rpt) **10.0** The Prisoner *Living in Harmony Western series starring Patrick McGoohan and Alexei Sayle.* (Rpt) **11.0** The Prisoner *Once Upon a Time Leo McKern stars as a man on the verge of a nervous breakdown as he is tortured to death by a villainous prisoner.* (Rpt) **12.0pm** The Prisoner *The Chimes of Big Ben Drake finds himself back home but everything is not what it seems as usual.* (Rpt) **1.0** The Prisoner *It's Your Funeral Can Prisoner stop an assassination from happening. NO!. Because it's a trap.* (Rpt) **2.0** The Prisoner *The Girl Who Was Death Drake is sent on a mission and confronts a meglomaniac who is obsessed with Napolean played by Welsh comic Kenneth Griffith.* (Rpt)

3.0 The Prisoner *Koroshi The Prisoner is sent to Japan to investigate the death of an agent. With Yoko Tani* (Rpt)

4.0 ITV Wrestling *Kent Walton with live bouts from Nuneaton Town Hall.*

6.0 The Prisoner *Arrival A secret agent finds himself in a colourful Welsh village. Stars Patrick McGoohan and Paul Eddington.* (Rpt)

7.0 The Prisoner *Fall Out McGoohan finds himself in a race against time to complete his commitment to Lew Grade.* (Rpt)

8.0 The Prisoner *The Schizoid Man Number six confonts an evil twin brother. Stars Patrick McGoohan and features Patrick McGoohan as himself.* (Rpt)

9.0 The Prisoner *The General Programme for schools.* (Rpt)

10.0 The Prisoner *Hammer Into Anvil Spy thriller* (Rpt)

12.0am The Prisoner *Arrival More lazy strip-schedulling with a programme that costs peanuts to broadcast. (Rpt - Ad Nauseum)*

ITVBen

10.0pm - Ben Shephard delights viewers with his wit and charm

6am Ben Shephard (Rpt)
7.0 Ben Shephard (Rpt) **8.0** Ben Shephard (Rpt) **8.30** Ben Shephard (Rpt) **9.0** Ben Shephard

9.30 CITV *Programmes for younger viewers presented by Ben Shephard including* **9.05** Ben Shephard **9.10** Ben Shephard (4/24) **9.25** Ben Shephard **9.45** Ben Shephard (Rpt)

10.0 Ben Shephard *Live discussion programme featuring Ben Shephard*

12.15pm News *with Ben Shephard*

12.30 Ben Shephard Omnibus *Catch up on last week's episodes.*

2.45 Ben Shephard *with Ben Shephard* **3.45** Ben Shephard (Rpt) **4.50** Ben Shephard (SL. Rpt)

5.30 Ben Shephard *Classic comedy* (Rpt)

6.0 Ben Shephard *Presented by Ben Shephard.*

7.0 Ben Shephard *Ben Shephard stars in the popular gameshow that features contestants as well.*

8.15 Ben Shephard Live *Live from the ITV Studios in Pergatory.*

10.00 The Ben Shephard News *All of today's Ben Shephard headlines read by Ben Shephard.*

10.15 The Ben Shephard Show *Join Ben as he welcomes some of the world's A list celebrities onto his sofa for a chat. Tonight's guest includes Ben Shephard.*

11.15 Late Night Ben *with Ben Shephard. Alone.*

12am Closedown

12.02 Not Really
You've Got Another Six Hours Of This Until It Starts All Over Again.

tv kack streaming guide
Reccommendered

Joan Hickson fighting crime on the moon in **Miss Marple in Space**

Paramount+

FANTASY

NEW Star Trek - Catspaw
· *available from Wed 30 Feb*

It's the Star Trek spin-off that all Trekkies have been waiting for as Kaftan and Kolob from the classic 60s episode Catspaw return in a new series of thrilling adventures as they explore the galaxy of the future using their own particular brand of black magic.

Disney

CARTOON

NEW K9 and the Time Babies
· *available from Wed 30 Feb*

Doctor Who's Disney takeover continues with this new animated series for the youngsters and the young-at-heart. The Time Lord's trusty robot dog is brought out of retirement by the high council of Gallifrey and entrusted with the protection of five Time Babies fresh from the Loom. But the renegade Omega wants them destroyed and K9 goes on the run with them. The five babies are Rodan, Cuk, Anan, Shada and The Moop - five cute characters who just can't keep out of trouble and are sure to be a big hit with the kids. **John Leeson** is the voice of K9 though the US version features **William Shatner** in the same role. New episodes drop on Wednesdays unless there is an 'R' in the month, in which case it's Tuesdays (or Thursday).

Netflix

CRIME DRAMA

NEW Blakey
· *available from Thu 31 Feb*

Ryan Murphy's much anticipated ten-part drama chronicling the early life of the infamous bus inspector finally makes its UK debut on Netflix. And it's a stunner! **Evan Peters** stars as the fresh young bus driver straight out of Luxton Bus College but his life is charged with tragedy as his fiance is struck down by a serial killer. Whilst he lashes out at his friends and colleagues, his mind is focussed on one thing - revenge! **Christopher Walken** cameos as the elderly Blakey relating his story to a young journalist (**Gugu Mbatha-Raw**) from his cell on death row.

MUSICAL POLITICS

NEW Truss - The Musical
· *available from Mon 33 Feb*

The hit West-End production comes to Disney. **Dominic Cooper** is Boris Johnson, **Emma Watson** is Liz Truss and **Ashton Kutcher** is Rishi Sunak in the heart-rending story of one woman's 49 day nightmare as she bears witness to some of the darkest economic attrocities this side of the WHSmith winter sale. Some great foot tappers! And the songs are pretty good too. Features **Chas 'n' Dave**.

Amazon Prime

FILMS

NEW The Road to Bali
· *available from Fri 32 Feb*

Bob Hope and **Bing Crosby** are the hapless stars of this comedy 'road' movie. As you'd expect from the streaming giant, Amazon have managed to source a rare 16mm pan and scan copy of the film from a VHS collection during a house clearance in Swansea. The colour has to be seen to be believed and some of the musical numbers can also be heard on occasion.

COMEDY

NEW The Lucy Show
· *available from Fri 32 Feb*

A chance to see the queen of US sitcoms in her fallow years with around eleven classic editions of the show. Along for the ride with **Lucille Ball** are guest stars including **Truman Capote, William Hartnell, Spiro Agnew** and **Lassie.**

SACRILEGIOUS

NEW Nineteen Eighty-four in color
· *available from Fri 32 Feb*

The original 1991 colorization of the classic BBC serial specially edited into a special 75 minute TV movie and placed on the streaming service by a shady American company in the mistaken assumption that every-thing black & white and without a © date on it is in the public domain. **Warning:** Colours made cause blindness.

Brickbox

CRIME DRAMA

NEW Miss Marple in Space
· *available from Mon 35 Feb*

Using the latest fake deep technology, the original BBC adventures of Agatha Christie's elderly amateur detective have been given a futuristic boost and sees **Joan Hickson** blasted into space where she puts her laser-sharp sleuthing skills to work solving murders on the European moonbase.

CRIME DRAMA

NEW Black Smith

Tom Smith is the local blacksmith in the quaint permanently sunny English village of Gennerick. He's also a master detective and when he's not shoeing horses or making shovels, he's out solving murders. If the local police are in trouble with ironmongery-based crimes, they always call on "Black Smith" for assistance whether they like it or not with hilarious outcomes. Stars **Joe Swash, Patsy Palmer** and **Nick Berry** as Inspector Grudge.

Big Brother is watching you... IN COLOUR Yvonne Mitchell, Peter Cushing and Andre Morell star in the classic BBCtv production of Nineteen Eighty-four

GREAT TV IS BRICKING IT

GET YOUR STINKIN' PAWS OFF ME YOU DAMN DIRTY APE!

ARE YOU BEING SERVED ON THE PLANET OF THE APES

Grace Brothers MEN'S WEAR

brickbox
CREATED BY BBC & itv

FILMATION's AVENGERS™

PADDINGTON in

brickbox
CREATED BY BBC & itv

BEAR 90

MOST SPECIAL BEAR

brickbox

CREATED BY BBC & itv

The Ancient Art of Putting the 13TH Dr WHO onto the Covers of Old Radio Times

Radio Times (Incorporating World-Radio) October 2 2018.

OCTOBER 6-12

Radio Times

SIXPENCE

LONDON AND SOUTH-EAST

BBC-1

tv

BBC-2

NEW FOR SUNDAY EVENING ON BBC-1

JODIE WHITTAKER time travels to new adventures

POLICE BOX

Dr WHO

on page 7

Radio Times (Incorporating World-Radio) October 2 2018.

OCTOBER 6-12

Radio Times

SIXPENCE

LONDON AND SOUTH-EAST

BBC-1

tv

BBC-2

GCHQ

DR WHO AND THE DALEKS

SUNDAY TV

Radio Times (Incorporating World-Radio) February 11, 1965 Vol. 166 No. 2154

FEBRUARY 13—19

Radio Times

SIXPENCE

LONDON AND SOUTH-EAST

BBC-1

tv

BBC-2

DR. WHO battles the Scorpion Queen

SEE PAGE 3

Radio Times *Incorporating World-Radio* February 13, 1965 Vol. Vol. No. 2964

Radio Times *tv*

FEBRUARY 13—19

BBC-1
BBC-2

SIXPENCE

LONDON AND SOUTH-EAST

DALEKS ARE BACK ON BBC-1

Radio Times (Incorporating World-Radio) October 2 2010

Radio Times *tv*

OCTOBER 6-12

BBC-1
BBC-2

SIXPENCE

LONDON AND SOUTH-EAST

DR. WHO

and her friends face their
old enemies, the Judoon

SUNDAY BBC-1   see page 3

Radio Times October 1987 MIDLANDS AND EAST ANGLIA

Radio Times *BBC tv*

JANUARY 20-26

THE
MONSTROUS
WORLD OF
DOCTOR WHO
see centre pages

RADIO TIMES EAST ART 1974

London and South-East
Edition

RadioTimes

Programes for
3-9 January: Ninepence

The Woman Who Fell To Earth
The Ghost Monument

Rosa
Arachnids in the UK
The Tsuranga Conundrum
Demons Of The Punjab
Kerblam!
The Witchfinders
It Takes You Away
The Battle of Ranskoor Av Kolos
Resolution

Can You Hear Me?
The Haunting Of Villa Diodati
The Last Cyberman part one
The Last Cyberman part two
2020 Holiday Special

Who?
Jodie Whittaker
as Dr.Who

Sundays BBC1 Colour

SOUTH 4-10 January One Shilling/5p BBC Radio West

Call the Midwife
Sunday BBC1

Grantchester
Friday ITV

Deadwater Fell
Friday Channel 4

RadioTimes

Silent Witness
Monday BBC1

Death in Paradise
Thursday BBC1

Father Brown
Weekdays BBC1

GREAT NEW DOCTOR WHO ADVENTURE! SUNDAY BBC1

THE RETURN OF THE MASTER

DOCTOR WHO

WHO'S THAT GEEZER, DOC??

HE'S MY OLDEST ENEMY

I'M USUALLY REFERRED TO AS THE MASTER!

LONDON 13 - 19 April 2019 Price £2.80 BBC Radio London

Adrian Dunbar's
retreat from
the Line of Duty

Colour interview - pages 6, 7

The Queen who
started it all!
TV's latest historical saga features
Queen Victoria. Your guide - page 8

RadioTimes

All you need to
know about
Hot Going Out
Lee Mack interview - pages 14-16

Game of Thrones -
eight years on and
still trail blazing

Colour feature - pages 58, 59

The Daleks are back!

YOU ARE THE DOCTOR...
YOU ARE AN ENEMY OF THE DALEKS!
YOU WILL BE EXTERMINATED!!

INSIDE:
Who are the Daleks?
Where do they come from?
What makes them tick?
How you can win a Dalek
Dr Who - Resolution of
the Daleks: BBC1 Colour

A-MT - AFTER FRANK BELLAMY

BRISTOL (BBC Radio page 78) 16-29 December 2017 Price £5

HAPPY
CHRISTMAS
SEASONS GREETINGS

RadioTimes

Which Doctor is Who?

INSIDE: All is explained
as Dr Who returns
Christmas Day BBC1 Colour

www.andystriner54.blogspot.com

SOUTH WEST BBC Radio West 8-14 February 2020 Price 5p

RadioTimes

Who's your friend?

Page 6: Michael Parkinson, Paul Jones and two photo-
shopped kids say why they'll be turning on to
Dr Who, Sunday BBC1 Colour

SOUTH WEST (BBC Local Radio West: page 78) 8-14 February 2020 Price 28p

RadioTimes

Who's Who?

Doctor Who's return to Gallifrey is celebrated
by 'The Five Doctors' who again face their enemy The Master
in a special feature-length story on BBC1.
Inside: companions in space . . . a Who Who's Who

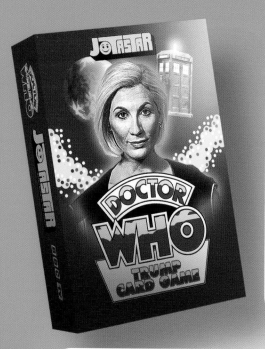

GIANT SPIDERS OF SHEFFIELD

MENTAL ABILITY:	2
SPECIAL POWERS:	**3**
WEAPONS:	5

These were ordinary house spiders grown to giant proportions through the actions of US businessman Jack Robertson who buried illegal toxic waste underneath his new hotel just outside Sheffield city centre. Dr Who suffocated them to death.

GRACE O'BRIEN

MENTAL ABILITY:	7
SPECIAL POWERS:	**5**
WEAPONS:	3

Grace is Ryan Sinclair's grandmother and following the death of his mother in 2012, she brought up grandson Ryan in the absence of his dad. Graham is her second husband. She met him whilst working as a nurse when Graham was recovering from cancer treatment. She was killed when Dr Who arrived in Sheffield.

THE FUGITIVE DOCTOR

MENTAL ABILITY:	8
SPECIAL POWERS:	**6**
WEAPONS:	8

Disguised as Gloucester tour guide Ruth Clayton, the so-called fugitive Dr Who was an incarnation of Dr Who that Dr Who herself was wholly unaware of. Despite the mystery over her heritage, Dr Who failed to uncover anymore details about it until the Master told her the full story when he turned up on a devastated Gallifrey in the far future.

BENNI AND VILMA

MENTAL ABILITY:	6
SPECIAL POWERS:	**3**
WEAPONS:	3

Benni and Vilma were tourists at the Tranquility resort on Orphan 55. During an attack by the Dregs, Benni was taken. Whilst searching for him outside the safety of the holiday complex, Vilma heard Benni's voice. He proposed to her and then asked to be killed as the Dregs were holding him hostage. Tragic isn't it?

DEAN

MENTAL ABILITY:	3
SPECIAL POWERS:	**1**
WEAPONS:	6

Dean was picking out the salad from his doner kebab when he met Tim Shaw. Thinking that the alien warrior was an early trick-or-treater, he proceeded to throw bits of tomato and cucumber at him. His last words were "Eat my salad, Halloween!" Dr Who failed to save him.

CYBER DRONES

MENTAL ABILITY:	3
SPECIAL POWERS:	**4**
WEAPONS:	8

Cyber Drones are the recycled heads of Cybus Cybermen. When Dr Who and her friends tried to save the last vestiges of mankind from the Cyber empire, their defence was totally eliminated by a squadron of these flying attack heads despite arriving in plenty of time. The humans barely escaped with their lives.

THE MASTER

MENTAL ABILITY:	9
SPECIAL POWERS:	**7**
WEAPONS:	7

When the Master uncovered the truth about Dr Who's shameful past lives, he punished the Time Lords by destroying Gallifrey and creating a new race of Cyber Masters from their remains. He also had to tell Dr Who about her secret past as she hadn't uncovered anything since she encountered Ruth Clayton (alias the fugitive Dr Who).

UK DEFENCE DRONES

MENTAL ABILITY:	4
SPECIAL POWERS:	**4**
WEAPONS:	6

Created as tools for law enforcement by American businessman Jack Robertson from the remains of the Recon Dalek that attacked GCHQ in 2019. These robots were taken over by cloned Dalek mutants. Dr Who was rescued from space prison by Captain Jack to deal with them but was unable to and she ended up calling in the real Daleks to deal with them.

We've done all the novels...
Now it's time for the non-fiction!

The Doctor Who Cook Book
by Gary Downie
Read by MARY BERRY
(includes £10 Sainsbury's
meat voucher)

**The Doctor Who Programme
Guide**
by John Mark Officer
Read by SIR IAN McKELLEN
(Now includes some sixth Doctor stuff)

The Doctor Who Pattern Book
by Joy Gammon
Read by GOK WAN
(Includes giant poster featuring the
fabulous photos from the original book.)

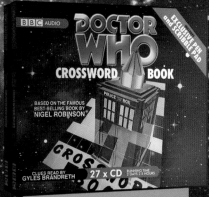

The Doctor Who Crossword Book
by Nigel Robinson
Read by GYLES BRANDETH
(Includes little Argos biro pen and mini
scribble pad.)

The Doctor Who Colouring Book
by Paul Crompton
Read by HANNAH GORDON
(Includes pack of six wax crayons.)

**Doctor Who – Great Bloody Battle
in Time/Space**
Read by GEORGE TAKEI
(The original Dr WHO novel translated
back into English from the rare Japanese
edition.)

Available on CD, Download, Vinyl, Tape, Wax Cylinder

DOCTOR WHO

Strawberry Flavour*
Candy Bar

Nastie's

DOCTOR WHO FIGHTS 'MASTERPLAN JINXX' part 1

DOCTOR WHO AND RUBY ARE VISITING THEIR OLD FRIEND PROFESSOR MASTERS IN THE QUIET VILLAGE OF DUNGSBLACK. THE ELDERLY PROFESSOR REVEALS HIMSELF TO BE NONE OTHER THAN THE SPACE CRIMINAL JINXX...

Doctor Who: Good grief! So you're the vile mastermind behind the kidnapping of all those innocent rabbits from the National Government Experimentation Centre!!!

QUICK AS A FLASH, DOCTOR WHO DRAWS HIS SPACE GUN AND SHOOTS THE DASTARDLY VILLAIN DEAD. HE QUICKLY FINDS THE RABBITS AND RETURNS THEM SAFELY TO THE CENTRE SO'S THAT HE AND RUBY CAN CONTINUE ON THEIR AMAZING TRAVELS...

INGREDIENTS: Lamb Powder (3%), Artificial Milk Powder (1.5%), Artificial Sweetner

*Artificial strawberry flavouring not suitable for vegetarians

Nastie's
DOCTOR WHO
Strawberry Flavour
Candy Bar

DOCTOR WHO CARTOON COLLECTION PICTURE No 2

3p

READ THE EXCITING CARTOON SERIAL ON THE BACK OF THE WRAPPERS!

ABOUT THE AUTHOR

Andrew-Mark Thompson's first *Doctor Who* memory is of Jon Pertwee ripping a policeman's face off at the end of part two of 'Terror of the Autons' in 1971. He was seven years old. He really became a fan though in 1976 when, during a fortnight's family holiday on a Great Yarmouth caravan site, he refused to go down to the beach and stayed in his bunk to read a Target book, Gerry Davis's *Doctor Who and the Cybermen*, which he'd just bought from the camp shop for 35p. By the decade's end, a whole array of Target novelisations adorned his bedroom bookshelf, forming a rainbow row of spines. During the 1980s he did all those things that young fans of TV series tend to do, including joining a fan club, editing a fanzine (or two) and being interviewed on local radio every time a new Doctor or companion was announced. But above all, he formed his outlook on the world through his love of a silly old British sci-fi TV show that, by the close of the '80s, was becoming neglected by others less open to its charms.

When the show was cancelled in 1989, he ran away and joined a circus (or rather a theme park, but a circus sounds more romantic). There he exercised his need for artistic expression by performing in Wild West shoot-outs and Hollywood stunt shows. He also assisted Sooty in putting on shows for several years, until their relationship deteriorated. As the new millennium dawned, he shifted his horizons. Having won a university scholarship in a local newspaper competition, he went all poor for three years, living off Pot Noodles and the kindness of strangers. Exiting the university with what is commonly called a degree, he realised he could have a career writing film and TV scripts. Instead, he started using a PC to make images of things that didn't exist. Following a messy nervous breakdown in the very public arena of a telephone call centre, he retreated into his own little world and began designing Target book covers for *Doctor Who* stories that hadn't yet been novelised; luckily, the BBC had seen his predicament and begun creating new stories in 2005.

By 2022, when he finally stopped creating his retro Target covers, his work had drawn much attention, and all the big publishers were clamouring for a piece of his creative genius. But, being a quiet and reflective soul, he shunned those lucrative offers in favour of one put to him by a small independent press. The result is now in your hands (or it may be open on a desk or a table, I don't know!): a book, with pages, a cover and everything. There's fun and madness. There's tragedy and sadness. There's even that smell that all modern books have when your first open them. Go on, have a sniff! Above all, this is A BOOK. A book that Andrew-Mark Thompson has written and designed. And it's the long-term consequence of a seven-year-old witnessing Jon Pertwee rip a policeman's face off in 1971. Who said kids are influenced by what they see on TV?

Andrew Mark-Thompson isn't married and doesn't own two cats.

The Shoemaker and the Elves

Retold by Sue Arengo
Illustrated by Omar Aranda

Contents

OXFORD
UNIVERSITY PRESS

Who's this? It's
the shoemaker.
The old shoemaker.

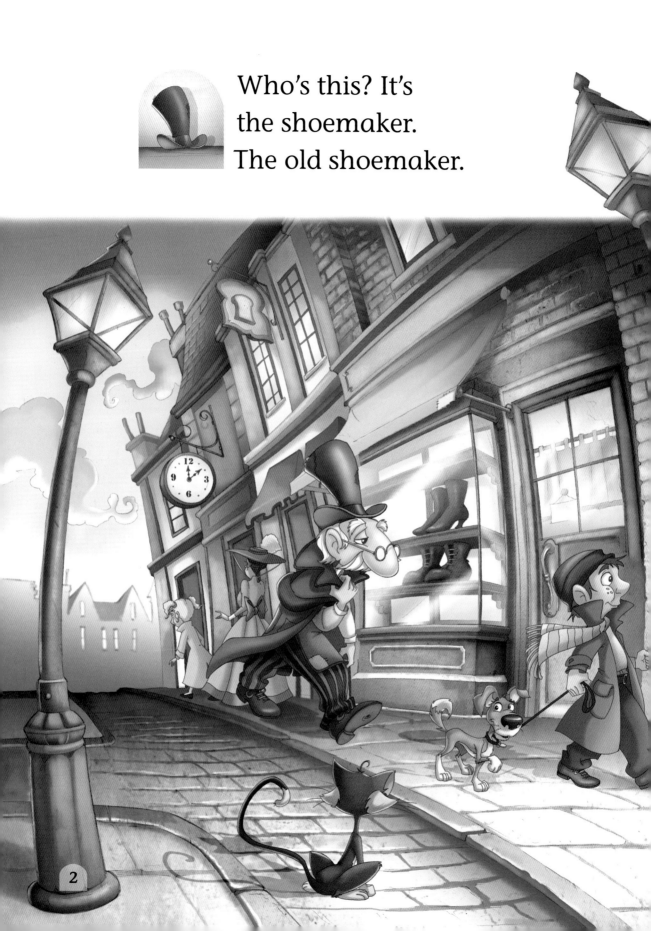

And here's his shop. The old shoe shop.

It isn't a very good shop. It doesn't make much money.

'One last pair of shoes,' says
the old shoemaker. 'That's all
I can make.'

'It's late,' says his wife. 'Make
them in the morning.'

In the morning they come down.
There's something on the table!
It's the shoes!

'Look!' cries the shoemaker. 'Magic!'

He puts the shoes in the window.
A lady sees them.

'Ah, Shoemaker,' says the lady.
'What beautiful shoes! I must buy
them. Here are three gold coins.'

'Three gold coins!' says the shoemaker. 'I can make more shoes now. Two more pairs.'

He goes out and he buys some more leather.

'I have some money,' he says. 'Look! Three gold coins!'

Look! Three gold coins!

'Two more pairs of shoes,' says the shoemaker. 'I can make two more pairs now.'

'It's late,' says his wife. 'Make them in the morning.'

It's late.

8

In the morning they come
down. There's something on
the table! Two pairs of shoes.

'Look!' cries the shoemaker.
'More magic!'

He puts the shoes in the window.
A man sees them.

'Ah, Shoemaker,' says the man.
'What beautiful shoes! I must buy
them. Here are six gold coins.'

Here are six gold coins.

'Six gold coins!' says the
shoemaker. 'I can make more
shoes now. Three more pairs.'

He goes out and he buys some
more leather.

'Look!' he says. 'I have some
money. Six gold coins!'

'I can make three pairs of shoes,'
says the shoemaker.

'It's late,' says his wife. 'Make
them in the morning.'

In the morning they come down.
There's something on the table!
Three pairs of shoes.

'Look!' cries
the shoemaker.
'Magic again.'

A family sees the shoes.

'What beautiful shoes!' they say.
'We must buy them. Here are nine
gold coins.'

'Nine gold coins!' says the shoemaker.
'But ... who is making all these shoes?'

That night the shoemaker hides. He and his wife hide. And they wait.

At midnight they see two little elves!

The little elves run in. They jump onto the table.

'Here's the leather!' they say. 'Let's work! Let's make some beautiful shoes!'

All night they work. They work and work and work. The shoemaker and his wife watch.

Let's work!

In the morning the elves run away.
But there's something on the table.
Four beautiful pairs of shoes!

'Now we know,' says the shoemaker.
'We know who helps us.'

'Yes,' says his wife. 'Two little elves.
But what can we do for them?'

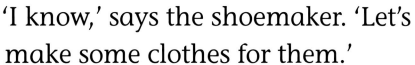

'I know,' says the shoemaker. 'Let's make some clothes for them.'

'Oh yes!' says his wife. 'Yes!'

17

Night comes. They leave the clothes on the table. Then they hide.

At midnight the little elves run in.

'What's this?' they say. 'Something for us? For us? Oh yes! It's something for us!'

They put on the new clothes and they dance. Dance, dance, dance!

It's something for us!

'Now it's time for us to go. Because they know! Because they know!' say the elves. 'Goodbye, Shoemaker!'

The elves never come back. But now the shoemaker makes good shoes. He works hard.

Now his shop is a good shop. And he is happy.

1 Write the words.

> two   pair   pairs   four   some   ~~one~~

1

_____one_____ shoe

2

a _____ of shoes

3

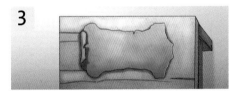

_____ leather

4

_____ gold coins

5

two _____ of shoes

6

_____ little elves

2 Circle the correct words.

1 The shoemaker's shop doesn't make much **(money)** / leather.
2 The lady buys the shoes because they are **old / beautiful**.
3 The shoemaker buys **shoes / leather** with the gold coins.
4 The elves work **at night / in the morning**.
5 The shoemaker and his wife make **shoes / clothes** for the elves.

3 What do they say? Write the words.

1

_____Three_____ gold _____ !

2

I can make two more _____ now.

3

Make them in the _____ .

4

Let's _____ !

4 Answer the questions. Write *Yes* or *No*.

1 Are the shoes beautiful? _____Yes._____
2 Are the shoes in the shop window? _____
3 Does a man see the shoes? _____
4 Does the lady buy them? _____
5 Does she buy them for two gold coins? _____

Picture Dictionary

buy

dance

clothes

elf   **elves**

coins

family

come back

gold *a gold coin*

come down

hard *He works hard.*

22

hide

midnight

jump

pair *a pair of shoes*

lady

run away

late *It's late.*

shoemaker

leather

watch

magic *magic shoes*

wife

Classic Tales

Classic stories retold for learners of English – bringing the magic of traditional storytelling to the language classroom

Level 1: 100 headwords
- The Enormous Turnip
- The Little Red Hen
- Lownu Mends the Sky
- The Magic Cooking Pot
- Mansour and the Donkey
- Peach Boy
- The Princess and the Pea
- Rumpelstiltskin
- The Shoemaker and the Elves
- Three Billy-Goats

Level 2: 150 headwords
- Amrita and the Trees
- Big Baby Finn
- The Fisherman and his Wife
- The Gingerbread Man
- Jack and the Beanstalk
- Thumbelina
- The Town Mouse and the Country Mouse
- The Ugly Duckling

Level 3: 200 headwords
- Aladdin
- Goldilocks and the Three Bears
- The Little Mermaid
- Little Red Riding Hood

Level 4: 300 headwords
- Cinderella
- The Goose Girl
- Sleeping Beauty
- The Twelve Dancing Princesses

Level 5: 400 headwords
- Beauty and the Beast
- The Magic Brocade
- Pinocchio
- Snow White and the Seven Dwarfs

All *Classic Tales* have an accompanying
- **e-Book with Audio Pack** containing the book and the e-book with audio, for use on a computer or CD player. Teachers can also project the e-book onto an interactive whiteboard to use it like a Big Book.
- **Activity Book and Play** providing extra language practice and the story adapted as a play for performance in class or on stage.

For more details, visit
www.oup.com/elt/readers/classictales

OXFORD
UNIVERSITY PRESS

Great Clarendon Street, Oxford, OX2 6DP, United Kingdom

Oxford University Press is a department of the University of Oxford. It furthers the University's objective of excellence in research, scholarship, and education by publishing worldwide. Oxford is a registered trade mark of Oxford University Press in the UK and in certain other countries

© Oxford University Press 2012

The moral rights of the author have been asserted

First published in Classic Tales 2000

2016 2015 2014 2013 2012

10 9 8 7 6 5 4 3 2

ISBN: 978 0 19 423882 3

This *Classic Tale* title is available as an e-Book with Audio Pack
ISBN: 978 0 19 423885 4

Also available: The Shoemaker and the Elves Activity Book and Play
ISBN: 978 0 19 423883 0

Printed in China

This book is printed on paper from certified and well-managed sources

ACKNOWLEDGEMENTS
Illustrated by: Omar Aranda/The Illustrators Agency